Starting Over with John and Yoko

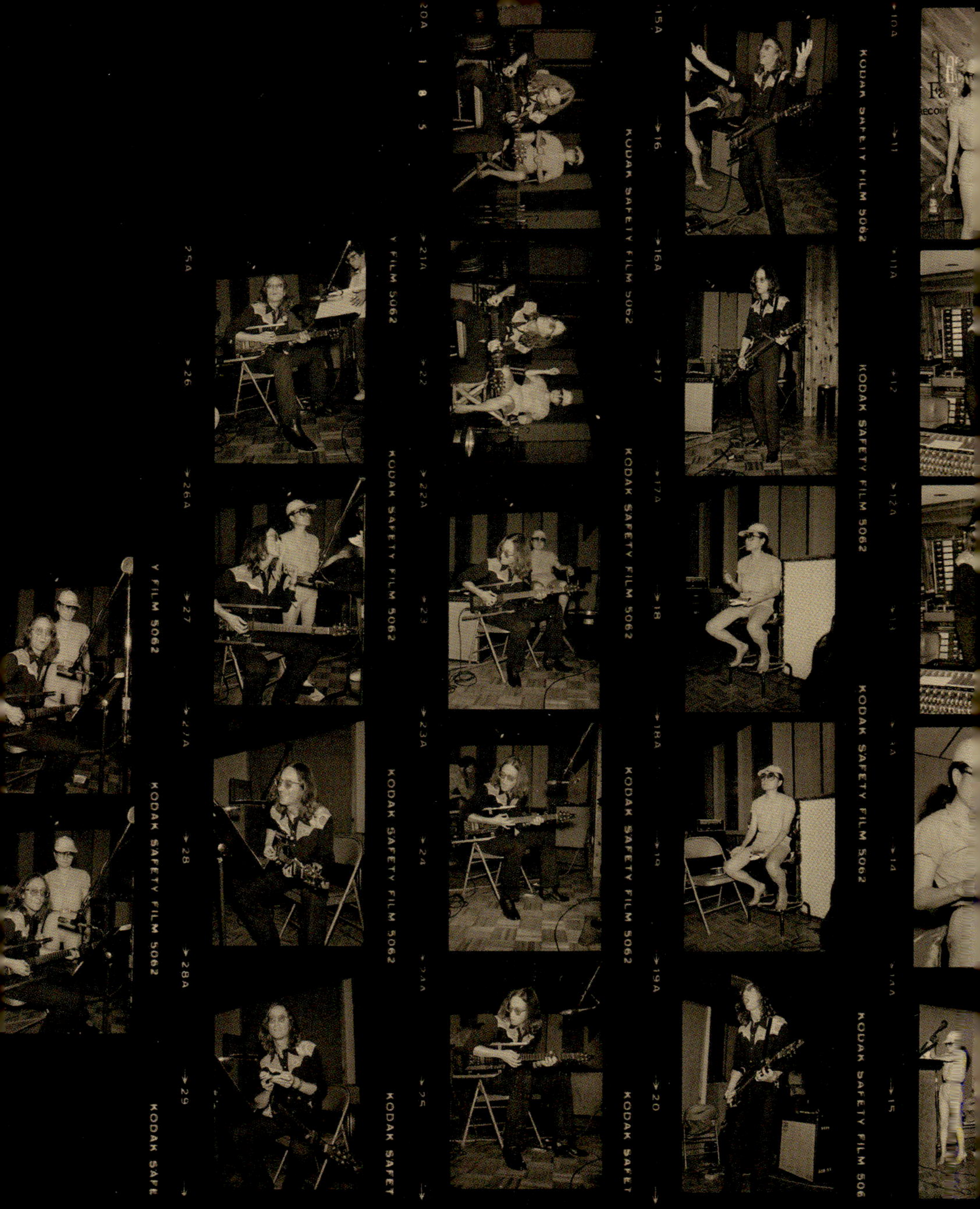
KODAK SAFETY FILM 5062

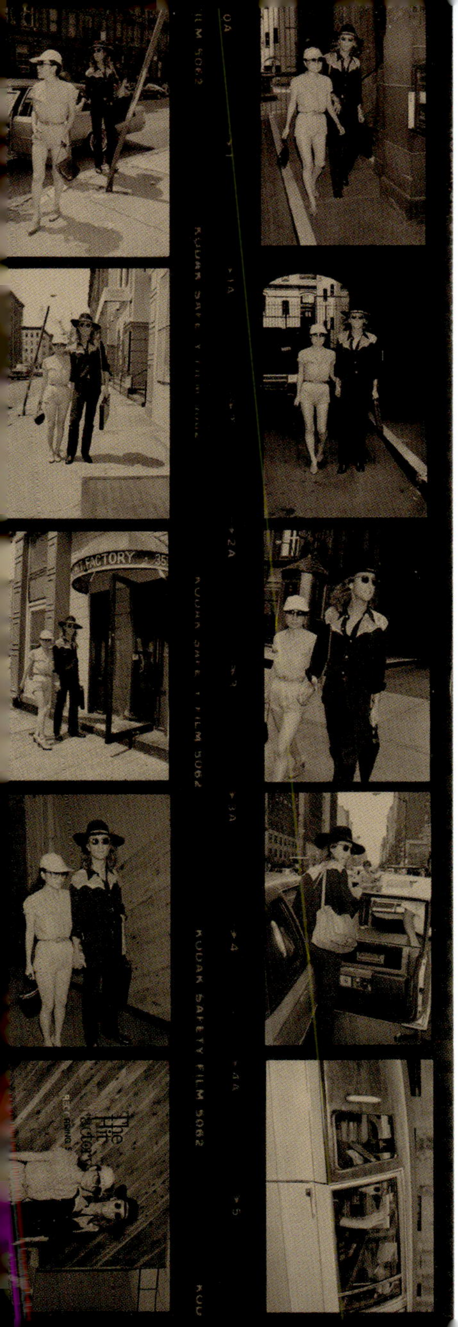

Starting Over with John and Yoko

The Photographs

Roger Farrington
and Kenneth Womack

RUTGERS UNIVERSITY PRESS

New Brunswick, Camden,
and Newark, New Jersey

London

Rutgers University Press is a department of Rutgers, The State University of New Jersey, one of the leading public research universities in the nation. By publishing worldwide, it furthers the University's mission of dedication to excellence in teaching, scholarship, research, and clinical care.

Library of Congress Cataloging-in-Publication Data
Names: Farrington, Roger author photographer | Womack, Kenneth author
Title: Starting over with John and Yoko : the photographs | Kenneth Womack and Roger Farrington.
Description: New Brunswick, New Jersey : Rutgers University Press, 2026. | Includes bibliographical references.
Identifiers: LCCN 2026000922 | ISBN 9781978844797 paperback | ISBN 9781978849211 hardcover | ISBN 9781978844803 epub
Subjects: LCSH: Lennon, John, 1940-1980 | Ono, Yōko | Rock Musicians—England | Artists—United States | Portrait photography—New York (State)—New York | LCGFT: Portraits | Biographies | Illustrated works
Classification: LCC ML420.L38 F35 2026 | DDC 782.42166092/2—dc23/eng/20260428
LC record available at https://lccn.loc.gov/2026000922

A British Cataloging-in-Publication record for this book is available from the British Library.

∞ The paper used in this publication meets the requirements of the American National Standard for Information Sciences—Permanence of Paper for Printed Library Materials, ANSI Z39.48-1992.

rutgersuniversitypress.org

For Colleen and Isabel

Joy comes not
through possession
or ownership but
through a wise and
loving heart.

—*Buddha*

Contents

Starting Over with John and Yoko

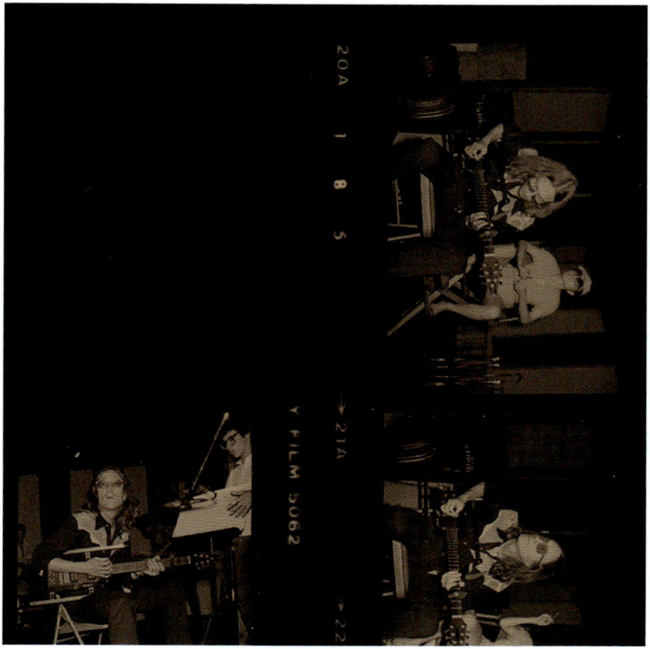

1.

Borrowed Time

History is rife with moments of poignancy and premonition—instances that, in hindsight, take on greater significance in light of the future course of human events. Ward Hill Lamon, Abraham Lincoln's former law partner and future biographer, understood this notion implicitly and would spend the balance of his life puzzling over this very phenomenon. As the sixteenth president's self-appointed bodyguard, Lamon was determined to protect his old friend at all costs. At the height of the Civil War, he had even taken to sleeping outside of the Lincoln Bedroom, wrapping himself in his cloak and leaning against the door to intercept any would-be assassins.

On Tuesday, April 11, 1865, Lamon met with the president and first lady, Mary Todd Lincoln, at the White House. According to Lincoln, some ten days earlier he had awoken from a dream that he simply could not shake—"somehow the thing has got possession of me, and like Banquo's ghost, it will not down." In the dream, Lincoln had been drawn to the East Room, where he was "met with a sickening surprise. Before me was a catafalque, on which rested a corpse wrapped in funeral vestments. Around it were stationed soldiers who were acting as guards; and there was a throng of people, gazing mournfully upon the corpse, whose face was covered, others weeping pitifully. 'Who is dead in the White House?' I demanded of one of the soldiers, 'The President,' was his answer; 'he was killed by an assassin.'" As if to reassure his friend—and perhaps to console himself—Lincoln later qualified his story, telling Lamon that "in this dream it was not me, but some other fellow that was killed. It seems that this ghostly assassin tried his hand on someone else."[1]

Before the week was out, the president dispatched Lamon to Richmond, Virginia, on an urgent matter pertaining to the end of the Civil War. That Friday night, as the President and Mrs. Lincoln settled in for the fateful performance of *Our American Cousin* at Ford's Theatre, Lamon was 140 miles away. Hence, the president's self-anointed protector was absent during John Wilkes Booth's moment of "phenomenal audacity" when the actor chose to assassinate Lincoln "in the presence of a vast concourse of admiring citizens."[2] Before he left Washington, D.C., Lamon had implored the president to avoid going out after dark—and especially not to the theater. It is natural, of course, to hypothesize in the wake of tragedy's aftermath when every instance and omen looms large, suddenly imbued with significance outside of the bounds of everyday life.

When it came to the terrible events of December 8, 1980, John Lennon harbored his own premonitions about an early, even violent demise. While he had spoken with wife Yoko Ono and producer Jack Douglas about his fears of an impending death in recent weeks, he had grown philosophical about the concept of no longer existing in the corporeal world. A few days earlier, during a pause in the playback sessions for Ono's "Walking on Thin Ice," Lennon shared a late brunch with the *SoHo Weekly News*' John Miller at Wylie's, an upscale East Side restaurant. John spoke animatedly about *Double Fantasy*, his new album with Ono, before launching into a lengthy conversation about death. "I used to worry about death when I was a kid," said Lennon. "Now the fear of it means less and less to me."[3]

A few days later, on the afternoon of Monday, December 8, Lennon and Ono were interviewed by RKO Radio personality Dave Sholin, who

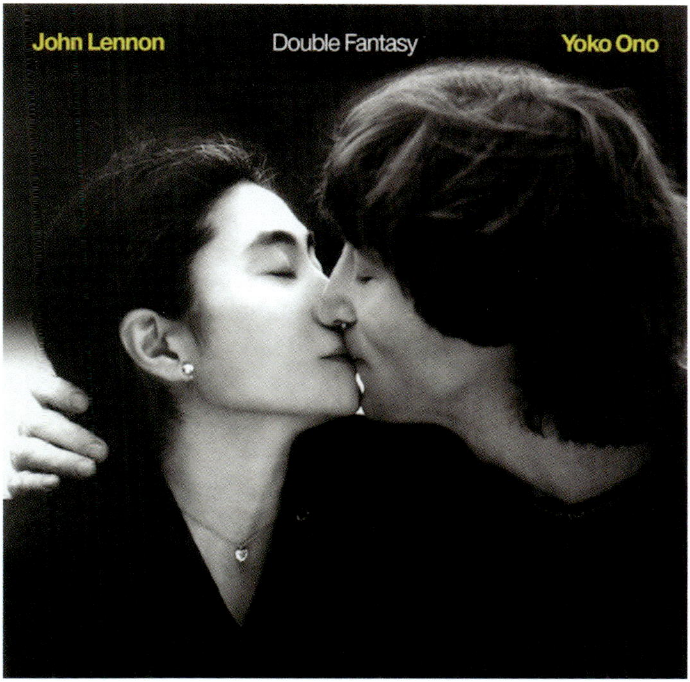

1. *Double Fantasy* album cover, Geffen Records, November 17, 1980.

had flown in from San Francisco the night before with scriptwriter Laurie Kaye, producer Ron Hummel, and Warner Brothers label rep Bert Keane. That afternoon, Lennon was buoyant, even optimistic, yet nevertheless working death into the conversation yet again. "I always considered my work one piece, whether it be with Beatles, David Bowie, Elton John, Yoko Ono," he told Sholin, "and I consider that my work won't be finished until I'm dead and buried, and I hope that's a long, long time."[4]

But none of this transpired until after a photograph had made its way around the world on the wings of the wire services. A grainy picture of John and Yoko in the doorway of the Hit Factory would be the calling card, the highly public announcement that the Lennons were going back into the studio to make a new album for the first time in five years. The project, which culminated with the November release of *Double Fantasy*, had actually begun four months earlier when the Lennons made the short drive from their residence in New York City's venerable Dakota apartment building, abutting Central Park and located on the Upper West Side, and the Hit Factory recording studio, a nondescript building on 48th Street between 8th and 9th Avenue.

The songwriting associated with the album had been underway for several months, if not years in some cases, with Lennon completing the compositions he intended to take into the studio the previous summer in Bermuda. That June, Lennon had even contrived the title of the couple's new album, a found object that he discovered in the Bermuda Botanical Gardens. "I was just walking in, and I looked down," John remembered, and a tiny sign under a cedar tree read, FREESIA, DOUBLE FANTASY. He was thunderstruck by the phrase. "I just thought, 'Double Fantasy'—that's a great title! 'Cause it has so many meanings that you couldn't even begin to think what it meant. So it means anything you can think of. It means double-couple."[5]

Working at the island's Fairylands Estate, Lennon also crafted several new songs, including "Woman," which would become a hit single in the new year, and "Grow Old with Me," which he composed in response to "Let Me Count the Ways," a song that Ono had written back in New York City and shared with him over the telephone. During his stay in Bermuda, for which he had been accompanied by his four-year-old son Sean and twenty-seven-year-old personal assistant Fred Seaman, the songs came fast and furious. "That's it!" he exclaimed during a particularly fruitful writing session. "'Living on borrowed time.' That's the phrase I've been looking for! I've had this song in my head for ages. It'll have a reggae beat, and I'll write the words around the theme of living on borrowed time, which is exactly what I've been doing. Or, come to think of it, what we're all doing, even though most of us don't like to face it."[6]

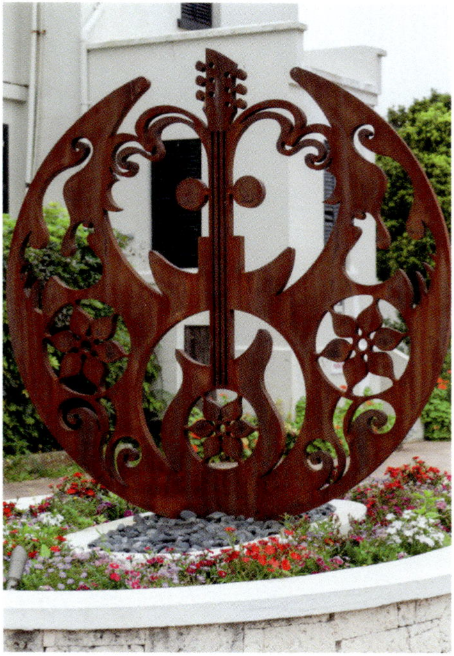

2. *Double Fantasy* sculpture, Bermuda Botanical Gardens.

It would be a sentiment that would pervade Lennon and Ono's songwriting over the final few months of his life. He had originally debuted "Gone from This Place" at the Hit Factory, having also recorded a demo of the song at the Dakota. With a tender acoustic guitar accompaniment, "Gone from This Place" found John embroidering a carefree song about the simple joys of living juxtaposed with an abiding fear of untimely death. And then there was "Walking on Thin Ice," which the Lennons had completed during the first week of December. A disco effusion about the risks and perils inherent in living—of "throwing the dice in the air"—Ono's "Walking on Thin Ice" seemed to epitomize the couple's dis-ease about the future.

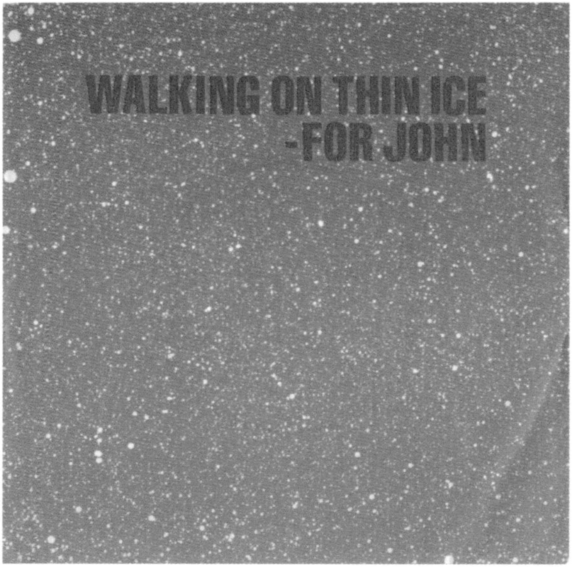

3. "Walking on Thin Ice" single cover, Geffen Records, February 6, 1981.

John and Yoko's highly visible return to public life was another matter altogether. The photograph that heralded Lennon's return to the studio for music lovers across the globe came from a very unlikely source. In a city rife with celebrity photographers, Ono had pointedly gone far afield when it came to hiring someone to document their August 7 arrival at the Hit Factory. And that someone was twenty-seven-year-old Roger Farrington, an up-and-coming Boston-area photographer who made his living snapping photos to publicize dance and theater events, along with the occasional wedding. Farrington had recently struck out on his own, founding Roger Farrington Photography after a five-year stint with the Charles Playhouse. A venerable theater a few blocks off the Common, the Charles was a 525-seat Off-Broadway venue in the heart of the city's theater district.

In 1975, a mere three months after graduating from Connecticut College, Farrington began working as company manager for the Playhouse. Owned by Frank Sugrue, the venue was a "four-wall-rental" professional

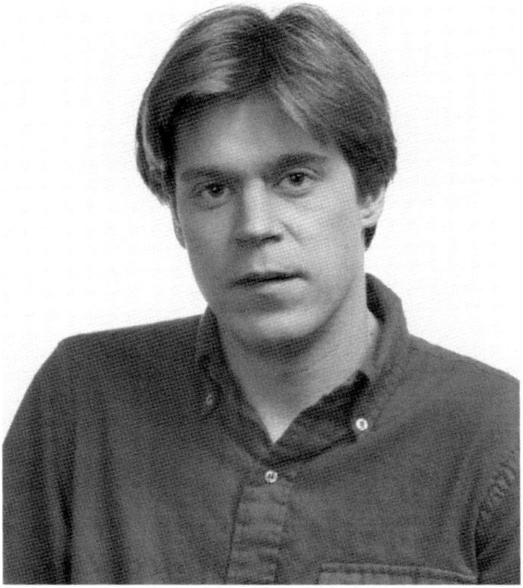

4. Roger Farrington, self-portrait, 1983.

theater struggling to keep the doors open. Back in those days, inner Boston was an entertainment and foodie backwater with very little in the way of nightlife, save for the emerging disco clubs in Kenmore Square, the Playboy Club and country and western–themed Hillbilly Ranch in Park Square, or the more infamous (and dangerous) Combat Zone strip joints and triple X movie houses on Washington Street. When it came to the restaurant scene, Bostonians contented themselves with traditional dishes served up at Locke Ober's (lunch only), Jacob Wirth's, Union Oyster House, Durgin-Park, or the revered Ritz-Carlton dining room. While Newbury Street boasted one or two after-work watering holes, popular nightlife meccas such as Faneuil Hall Marketplace, the Hampshire House "Cheers" bar, and the Lansdowne Street nightclub scene were still years away.

When it came to refined inner-city entertainment during that era, the Charles Playhouse was one of the city's few reliable options. "Whatever was cool about Boston nightlife was usually happening at the Charles,"

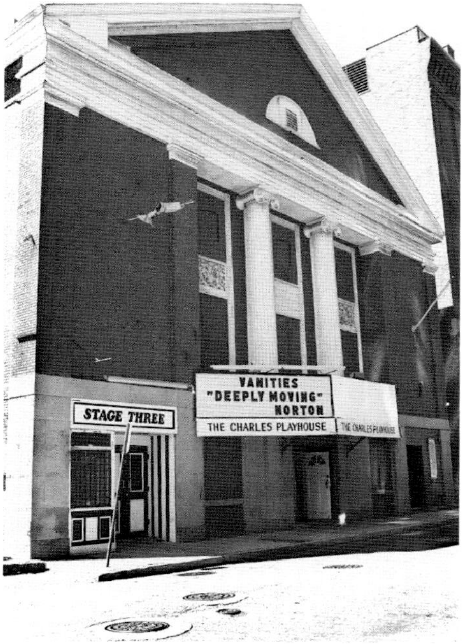

5. The Charles Playhouse, ca. 1976.

Farrington later recalled. "My jobs there included box office, company managing, publicity photography, and eventually running the entire complex as Mr. Sugrue's assistant." The playhouse catered to a wide and discerning audience. The complex featured a popular 100-seat bar and comedy club, the aforementioned 525-seat mainstage on the upper level, and a 125-seat cabaret theater and bar downstairs. Working at the playhouse forced Farrington to serve as a jack-of-all-trades. No job was too big or too small—whether it meant wrangling kiddie performers for Sunday matinees or taking a turn behind the drum kit as a performer in *Young Country*, a bicentennial children's musical.

Eager to expand the playhouse's reach, Sugrue hired thirty-eight-year-old Charles J. Cohen to conduct the theater's PR duties. Having founded his own firm in 1962, Cohen conducted a wide array of PR activities associated with the city's sports and theater events, as well as providing pay-to-play coverage for its various restaurant and theatrical openings. Incorporated as Advertising & Entertainment, Cohen's office was located at 25 Huntington Avenue in Boston's Back Bay neighborhood. For his part, Sugrue was a big fan of Cohen's off-beat approach to theatrical publicity. Back in the 1960s, Cohen had served as business manager for Cape Cod's Provincetown Playhouse, the famed venue that was the home of the Provincetown Players. The company's roster was the stuff of literary legend, featuring such names as Djuna Barnes, Theodore Dreiser, Edna St. Vincent Millay, Wallace Stevens, and perhaps most notably, American playwright Eugene O'Neill. During his days with the Provincetown Playhouse, Cohen helped the company find its niche as an artistic destination beyond the glitz of Broadway. He even roomed for a time with Richard Gere, who starred in the Provincetown Players' edgy take on Tom Stoppard's *Rosencrantz and Guildenstern Are Dead*.[7]

When it came to the Charles Playhouse, Cohen and Sugrue hatched a plan to take advantage of the inner city's notorious reputation by way of Boston's blue laws. The expression "Banned in Boston," however hard to comprehend in today's permissive X-rated world, was a legal reality in Irish Catholic, conservative Boston from the 1930s through the early 1970s. In point of fact, Boston's infamous blue laws dated long before the Irish arrived, having roots in early 1630s New England colonial era when Boston was settled by English religious purists. More widely known as the Puritans, they practiced extreme religious intolerance, often convicting Quakers of heresy and hanging them publicly on the Boston Common.

Back in the 1960s and 1970s, Boston's blue laws were weaponized by the authorities to target legally defined obscenity in books, plays, live theater, and the arts in general. When Broadway's smash hit *Hair* opened at Boston's Wilbur Theatre in 1971, for instance, the vice squad closed the show during its famous nude scene. A Boston judge ruled that the

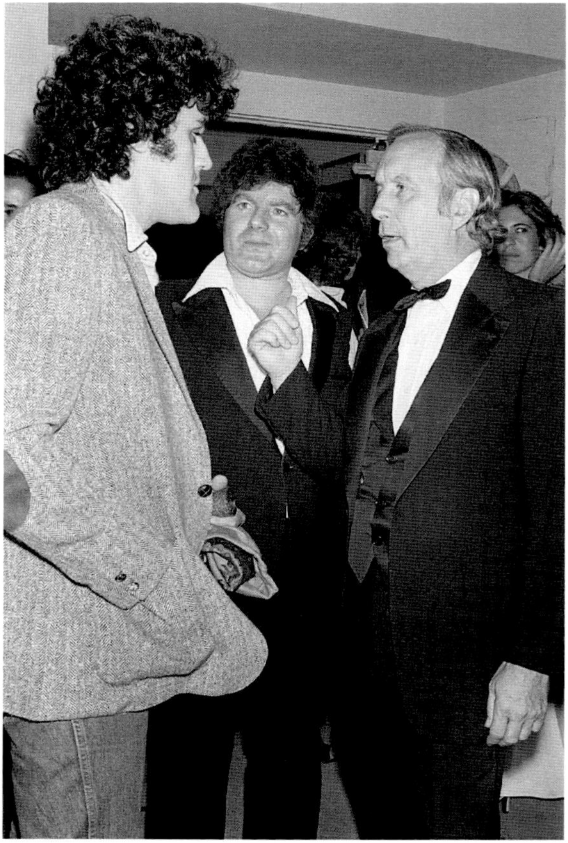

6. Jay Leno, Charles J. Cohen, and Frank Sugrue at the Charles Playhouse, 1979.

production could only continue if the actors wore skin-colored body suits during the law-breaking scene. Naturally, the "Banned in Boston" *Hair* controversy only led to long ticket lines at the Wilbur, greatly improving the show's bottom line. Not to be outdone, Cohen and Sugrue climbed aboard the "Banned in Boston" publicity-scam bandwagon. In 1973, Sugrue purposefully booked Terrence McNally's self-described "artistically erotic" play *Sweet Eros*.

Meanwhile, Cohen rolled out a bold publicity campaign. Adorning the show's press release with the high-minded rhetoric of First Amendment rights, artistic freedom, and freedom of expression, Cohen highlighted *Sweet Eros*'s unabashed artistic and tasteful depiction of full-frontal male and female nudity. Cohen papered local media outlets with the announcement, which he proudly hand-delivered to the Boston Police Department's Vice Squad along with invitations for front-row tickets for the show's opening night. When the cops took the bait, Cohen went full-throttle, tipping off the entire local press corps, wire services, and TV news crews and promising editors a jaw-dropping page-one story—something along the lines of "Vice Squad to Attend Opening Night Nudity!"

And as expected, the moment Boston's archaic laws were violated, undercover cops stood up in their seats waving their shiny badges. And while news cameras flashed and TV lights brightened the scene, they loudly announced, "Stop the show! This is the Boston Police. Actors onstage, do not move. You are under arrest. Audience must exit the theater immediately." For the grand finale, the cops climbed onstage, handcuffed the show's two nude actors, who themselves had been tipped off by Cohen and Sugrue, while stagehands helpfully provided blankets. By design, the opening frenzy associated with *Sweet Eros* resulted in a perfectly staged media event, continuing over several more days of courthouse reportage. Even the judge got in on the fun, letting the company off with a token fine, a promise to wear body suits, and a request for two free tickets. While Cohen, Sugrue, and the local media were laughing all the way to the bank, Massachusetts became the stuff of regional, if not national, embarrassment. Indeed, by the early 1980s, most of Boston's blue laws had been either ignored or abolished.

When Farrington first encountered Cohen a few years after the events associated with *Sweet Eros*, the PR flack's reputation preceded him. Farrington was well aware of the "Banned in Boston" gambit and its impact on the playhouse's fortunes. In his capacity as Sugrue's assistant, he knew that Cohen employed a couple of excellent Boston photographers to shoot the shows and stars he handled at the playhouse. After all, their huge black-and-white promo prints decorated the theater's lobby. Farrington's opportunity finally arrived when the producer of an incoming children's musical hired him to take publicity stills. During the production, Cohen observed Farrington shooting the event with his Nikon and asked if he did his own darkroom work. By the following winter, Cohen entrusted Farrington with handling the lion's share of the playhouse's photography, as well as with a number of celebrity photo shoots. Thanks to Cohen, Farrington's photos began appearing in a growing list of local papers and magazines.

In a particularly fortuitous moment, Farrington handled photography for the Off-Broadway musical *Diamond Studs*. Farrington's candid shot of New York senator Jacob Javits dancing onstage with his daughter Joy was picked up by the wire services, eventually running in *Time* magazine's popular weekly People feature. Quite suddenly, Farrington's freelance photography career had been launched. In short order, he began receiving inquiries both in Boston and beyond, snapping an array of celebrities, including Richard Chamberlain, Harvey Fierstein, Jay Leno, and Robert Preston.

Farrington's time at the playhouse was clearly coming to an end. For the young photographer, working at the Charles had lost its luster long ago. Serving as Sugrue's jack-of-all-trades had reached its limit. Farrington was exhausted after years of having to shoo area prostitutes out of the alleyways or observing Sugrue's mounting fears about the mafia's brazen effort to take over the playhouse. When it came to protecting the Charles's patrons, Sugrue hired a part-time security guard—a recent parolee who lived out of a beat-up van on Warrenton Street. Farrington was shocked to learn that the security guard's sidearm was quite literally a stage prop replica of a .38-caliber police special, which he planned to wield if the Charles ever devolved into a standoff. For Farrington, things came to a head when Sugrue, who had been working with off-book distributors to stock the bar, asked if he could put the photographer's name on his application for a liquor license.

At the onset of the summer of 1980, Farrington finally left the playhouse to open a full-time PR, editorial, and advertising photography business of his own. One of his first high-profile shoots was carried out at the behest of the royal Thai consulate. Prior to the assignment, he received a crash course in Secret Service and royal photography protocols. Acting as the queen of Thailand's official photographer for her seven-day royal visit to Boston, Farrington documented every aspect of the elegant, forty-eight-year-old Queen Sirikit's hectic schedule of lavish dinners, formal receptions, and informal meet and greets. Several key images of Farrington's were selected for placement in newspapers and magazines in Boston and Thailand.

Having completed the complex, high-profile assignment, Farrington proudly reveled in the successful launch of his new full-time photography business. He had gone into business for himself—and seemingly without a hitch. After taking a much-needed European vacation, which culminated in an extended jaunt on the beautiful Greek island of Hydra, Farrington returned to what would amount to the most unusual and impactful assignment of his career.

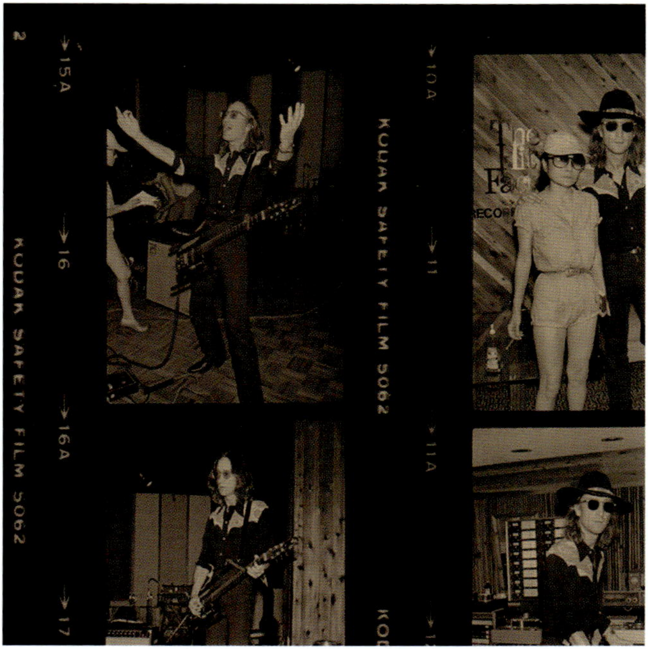

2.

Numbers Game

That same summer, as Farrington was relaxing in Europe, Cohen received a telephone call from Yoko Ono. When his assistant informed him that she was on the line, "I didn't believe it," he later recalled and told her to hang up the phone. Moments later, an undeterred Yoko called him back. "Mrs. Lennon was looking for a PR person who lived outside of New York City," said Cohen. When he learned that she had a project that she wanted to discuss with him, Cohen decided to make the trip down to New York City in fine style. "So I hired a Rolls Royce Silver Spur and motored to the Dakota apartments."[1] With his debilitating phobia about air travel, there was simply no way Cohen was taking the shuttle from Boston to New York City. Besides, he knew full well that he would be invoicing her for the car service down to the Dakota.

One of New York City's most treasured and enigmatic landmarks, the Dakota had been constructed in the early 1880s at the behest of Edward Clark, cofounder with Isaac Singer of the Singer Sewing Machine Company, the firm that had transformed the garment industry since the mid-century. Clark selected Dutch architect Henry Hardenbergh to bring his vision to life. For his part, Hardenbergh viewed his design for the Dakota as the opportunity to let his creative imagination loose on what, in good time, would surely emerge as one of the burgeoning city's most distinctive addresses. The result was a series of Old World European embellishments—high-pitched roofs and imposing balustrades pocked with chimneys, flagpoles, turrets, and finials. The Dakota's exterior was constructed of carved stone friezes, along with a dry moat that marked the building's perimeter and was decorated with the bearded face of Neptune entwined with a pair of serpents.

Legend has it that the building was bequeathed its unusual name because of its remoteness—that it was so distant from the city's hubbub that it might as well have been constructed in the Dakota Territory. In truth, the Dakota's name found its origins in Clark's passion for Native American lore and the nation's Western expansion into the territories during that era.[2] Nestled at the corner of Central Park West and West 72nd Street, the Dakota was an architectural wonder, standing out from the landscape, its spandrels and balustrades giving it a German Renaissance character, not to mention the fearsome sight of the menacing gargoyles that guarded its perimeter.[3] And then there was the imposing archway that opened onto West 72nd Street, the nineteenth-century building's main entrance, a porte cochere that had originally been constructed to admit horse-drawn carriages into the Dakota's cavernous central courtyard, elegantly fitted out with a pair of cast-iron fountains. In later years, a copper-plated sentry box would be erected on the western side of the archway.

The "John Lennons," as they were known among the Dakota's austere tenancy, had purchased their seventh-floor apartment in 1973, a year after the building had been added to the National Register of Historic Places. In 1976, the Dakota would be declared a National Historic Landmark. Since the late 1960s, the building had been lodged in the national consciousness when famed director Roman Polanski filmed the exterior shots for the supernatural thriller *Rosemary's Baby* and deployed the Dakota's imposing Gothic architecture to spine-tingling effect.

When he pulled up to the Dakota in his rented Rolls, Cohen was suitably impressed. Making his way past the sentry box and into the

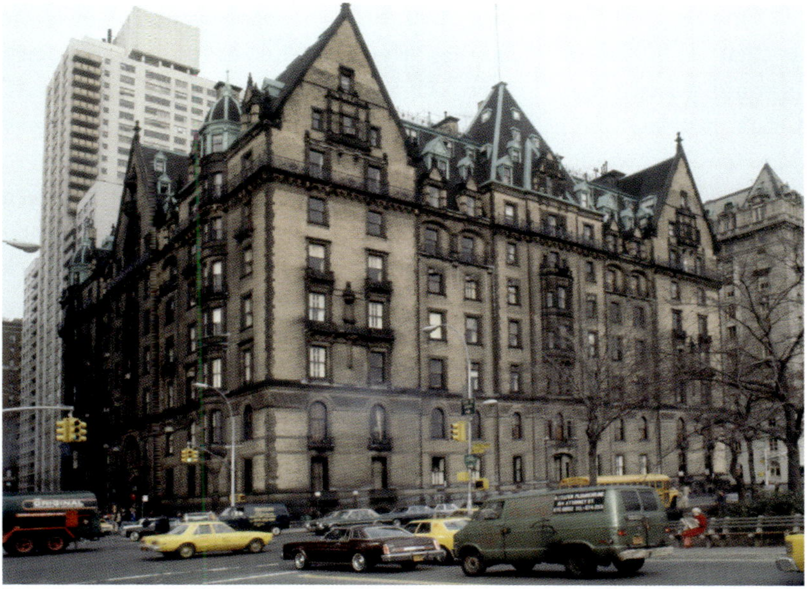

7. The Dakota, 1980.

porte cochere, the PR man was ushered into Yoko's first-floor office suite, which consisted of two high-ceiling rooms. Nicknamed Studio One by John and Yoko, the office served as the headquarters of Lenono Music, while doubling as Yoko's inner sanctum. The outer office served as the nerve center of the Lenono operation, with banks of white filing cabinets—anointed with labels such as "Royalties, BMI" and "Petty Cash"—towering over the room. Studio One's main room was dominated by a massive gold-inlaid desk set, along with an elaborate glass-covered coffee table, with serpents twisted about the legs situated below a trompe l'oeil painting on the ceiling of clouds scudding across a brilliant blue sky—in the process, quite literally, bringing Lennon's signature composition "Imagine" ("above us only sky") to life.[4]

Ono began the proceedings by running Cohen's numbers—his time and date of birth—to ensure that he was a karmic fit for the job she had in mind. "Seems that I passed," said Cohen. "At any rate, I was hired." Ono's motives were indubitably clear: hiring a PR firm from faraway Massachusetts would enable her plot to the Lennons' bravura return to public life without the notorious New York City press breathing down their necks. This would be a momentous occasion, to be sure—the first new offering from John since his *Rock 'n' Roll* LP, which was released back in February 1975.[5] Yoko intended to take full advantage of the moment. Her PR plans were twofold: first, she wanted Cohen to rehabilitate her own reputation. She was well aware that Beatles fans the world over blamed her for the group's disbandment. To that end, Yoko entreated Cohen to "spread the story that she raised Holstein cows, not for slaughter but for fresh milk, to make it appear as though she was the very milk of human kindness."[6] As he later explained to Farrington, Cohen was especially impressed with Yoko's professional acumen. "She's been investing all of John's Beatles money," he said laughing. "She's no dummy, you know. She's in control of everything and everyone. She went to Sarah Lawrence College in New York and comes from a very wealthy family."

In short order, Cohen would succeed in landing international headlines that celebrated Yoko's business savvy—namely, that her investments in prized Holstein cows had paid off handsomely with the sale of a dairy cow known as "Spring Farm Fond Rose" for a record-breaking $265,000. For the second part of her plan, Ono tasked Cohen with lining up a publicity photographer to document the Lennons' triumphant return to the studio later in the summer. The resulting photographs would illustrate Cohen's subsequent press release. Naturally, such assignments required the utmost secrecy. At the time, John was still in Bermuda, where he was putting the finishing touches on his latest batch of songs. Before he left the Dakota that day, Cohen—who admired luxury and wealth to a fault—managed to wrangle a tour of the Lennons' residence out of Yoko, who was happy to oblige. "She gave me a tour of their many apartments on multiple floors in the Dakota," he later recalled. "She took me into one huge storage room, and you wouldn't believe what's in there. It's like a Beatles museum, with tons of old Beatles stuff everywhere: John's guitars, amps, musical equipment, and racks of clothes—even the suit John wore on *The Ed Sullivan Show*—and a complete set of Ringo's drums!"

Back in Boston, Cohen wasted little time in contacting Farrington about handling the Lennons' photo-op. Farrington had recently returned from his six-week European jaunt, and he was anxious to get back to work. During his three weeks on Hydra, he had suffered two disappointingly fruitless celebrity photo opportunities, one with musician Leonard Cohen and the other with Hollywood movie star Peter Sellers. For the former, he had even staked out the singer-songwriter's private home. "Keeping a cool eye out for any sign of the 'Suzanne' singer's presence," he recalled. "Our plan was to have our attractive female friends invite the reclusive artist over for a glass of retsina. And after amusing him with our impressive knowledge of his poetry and music, we would all become fast friends and—with Leonard's blessings—I would shoot candid portraits and release my exclusive image and brilliantly written captions to worldwide media." But alas, it was not meant to be. The singer had been staying elsewhere that summer.

Farrington's attempt to capture Sellers's image also came to naught. The actor who portrayed the famously confused Inspector Clouseau of *The Pink Panther* films was living aboard a massive yacht that was moored nearby. "Disembarking down a gleaming gangway from the sleek, white yacht with a gorgeous blonde on his arm, the *Dr. Strangelove* star looked to me like a perfect Hollywood photograph in his crisp white suit, white fedora, white gloves, and black walking stick." With his camera at the ready, Farrington debated the merits of taking the actor's photo by ambush or simply approaching him outright. But then he noticed something wasn't quite right. "Sellers was walking slowly, possibly even supported by his escort's arm, his face looking pale, his body seeming extremely frail." Farrington nixed any further notions about photographing Sellers that day. Perhaps he would get another opportunity when

Sellers was healthy and hale? Sadly, less than a month later, the actor had died in London at age fifty-four, having succumbed to a heart attack.

Ensconced back in his Boston office a few weeks later, Farrington would never forget the lazy July morning when Cohen's sharp, nasally voice came on the line. "Have you ever heard of John Lennon and Yoko Ono?" he asked the photographer. "Yes," Farrington replied with feigned nonchalance. "Well, I might know of a little assignment for you," said Cohen, "if you want it." The conversation continued with an amazing job offer. "Now that you've finally returned from your vacation, I was wondering if you might possibly be available to meet the Lennons at their Dakota apartment in New York City—sometime in the next couple of weeks. It'll probably be on short notice, maybe even less than twenty-four hours, to take a few photos of John and Yoko leaving the Dakota and going into the recording studio to start work on a new record."

"BOOM. There it was," Farrington later recalled, "a once-in-a-lifetime incredible photo assignment!" Cohen quickly tempered the younger man's enthusiasm. "First of all, you can't tell anyone about any of this conversation. NO ONE must know. This is TOP SECRET. Yoko Ono insists on your promise of absolute secrecy." Lowering his voice, Cohen added another caveat. "And by the way, you don't exactly have the job yet. She's considering other photographers, but she likes you." And then Cohen backpedaled a little. "Anyway, there's no definite job right now," he added, "and all of this could go up in smoke. So don't get your hopes up."

For the life of him, Farrington could scarcely make sense of this opportunity, vague as it was. "Why me?" he wondered. "There must be a hundred photographers in New York that John and Yoko could hire; why do they want me—from Boston?" And just as significantly, "How did Charles Cohen get so famous to work with these major pop music stars? I go away for six weeks, and look what happens! What exactly was going on here?" And then there was Cohen's quip about whether Farrington had heard of John and Yoko.

When it came to the Beatles, Farrington was an early adopter. His older sister Lee had introduced him to the band. "'Have you HEARD the Beatles YET?' my flush-faced, wide-eyed sister shouted into my innocent face," he recalled. "'You HAVE to hear them. Just LISTEN! They have long hair, and they're from Liverpool,'" she cried as she dropped the needle and the first notes of "I Want to Hold Your Hand" blasted from the tiny speaker on her pink phonograph. Within days, Farrington would be one of the record-breaking seventy-three million viewers who tuned into their North American debut performance on TV's *Ed Sullivan Show* on February 9, 1964. He had been an ardent fan ever since, following their unparalleled achievements as they created one masterwork after another with *Rubber Soul, Revolver, Sgt. Pepper's Lonely Hearts Club Band, The White Album,* and *Abbey Road*. And Farrington certainly knew about John's marriage to Yoko, which the couple famously celebrated with a "bed-in" for world peace at the Amsterdam Hilton.

As he awaited Cohen's telephone call, Farrington understandably began to have doubts about the whole enterprise. He still couldn't wrap his mind around the idea that a small Boston agency with no experience in dealing with the international rock 'n' roll media corps would be selected to break the story about the Lennons' return to the studio. In his darkest moments, he began to wonder if Cohen was playing him—that Farrington was merely being solicited as a possible backup photographer. "Don't get your hopes up," Cohen had warned. After all, there was a bevy of world-class rock photographers working during that era. Virtual household names like Annie Leibovitz and Bob Gruen, who had taken the famous shot of Lennon donning his New York City T-shirt in the mid-1970s. There was one aspect that gave Farrington hope. Knowing Cohen's penchant for self-promotion, he was surprised by the PR flak's restraint in not leaking his good fortune to the Boston media. Was the John and Yoko photo shoot so hush-hush that Cohen had been sworn to abject secrecy? Perhaps this was the real thing after all.

A week had passed since Cohen's first, encouraging telephone call. In the interim, Cohen had landed international headlines with the Holstein cow story—"Ex-Beatle Wife Sells Cow for Auction Record." When he saw the item in *The Boston Globe,* Farrington took the opportunity to telephone Cohen. "Congratulations, Charles," he said. "Your instincts were right on. Yoko must have loved it." Always proud of his work, Cohen eagerly shared that "she loved it! She told me that John saw it in the morning papers and ran into her office waving the paper. He was telling everyone, 'Look how brilliant Mother is!'"

And that's when Cohen coyly announced that "Yoko was wondering if you could do something for her." To his surprise, Farrington learned that Yoko wanted him to carry out a basic copy job. "Yoko wants you to make copies of some photos of her with Sean and John," said Cohen. "Can you do that for her, please, Roger? You can charge her your usual rates." Farrington couldn't contain his surprise. "Surely, there are tons of photo labs in New York. Why does she want me to do it?" he asked. In response, Cohen delivered the usual refrain, "Don't ask any questions. Yoko is going to messenger an envelope to you today from New York. She wants to know how soon you can get it done. Can you do it by tomorrow?"

That afternoon, Farrington found himself in possession of the envelope. "I carefully opened the package, removing the protecting cardboard layers and pulling out two items," he recalled. "Immediately, I was disappointed by what I saw. The first was a very blurry, out-of-focus, black-and-white 8 × 10 glossy of what I assumed to be a naked John, naked Yoko, and naked Sean running hand-in-hand down a grassy hill in front of an equally blurry New England–style mansion. The other item was an even bigger disappointment. Rolling my eyes, I immediately recognized it as the *Two Virgins* album cover and its infamous portrait of John and Yoko in full-frontal nudity."[7] Farrington was now utterly confused. Was this copy job designed to assess the photographer's printing skills or some kind of loyalty test?

Allowing his professional ethics to dictate his response, Farrington called Cohen immediately and explained that he could not copy nude

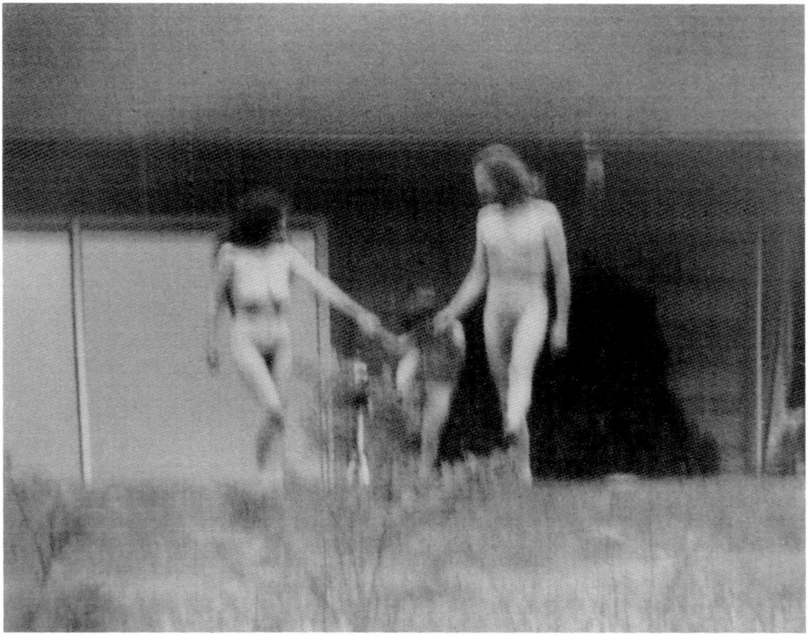

8. John, Yoko, and Sean Lennon copy job, July 1980.

photos without written permission from Yoko and/or the copyright owner. "After a few choice expletives, Cohen acknowledged my awkward position and said he would call Yoko for me," Farrington recalled. Within the hour, Cohen telephoned him back, reassuring him that Yoko would assume full responsibility. "Now," said Cohen, "will you please just copy the fucking photos?"

That same afternoon, Farrington dutifully produced negatives of the photos and developed sets of matching prints, neatly packaging them in glassine sleeves with cardboard backing. Yoko's driver picked them up not long afterward, leaving Farrington to wonder if he'd passed the test. Had this whole, strange business with Cohen been a fever dream? Or was it really going to happen?

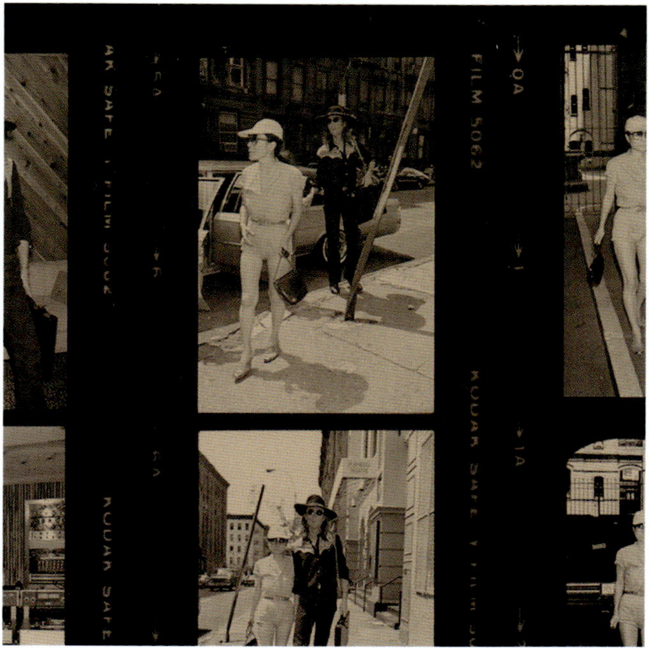
FILM 5062

3.

Stepping Out

At the end of their July telephone conversation, Cohen had told Farrington to "expect an important call at any time." But as the days went by, Farrington could no longer contain himself. "Letting extreme curiosity get the better of me, I called the office back to ask what was going on," he recalled. "I was afraid that the job might have gone elsewhere." When he finally spoke to Cohen, he asked, "Is this Lennon thing for real or what?" A clearly irritated Cohen replied that "I have no idea what that crazy Chinese woman is doing from one day to the next. She changes her fucking mind every minute!" After Farrington coolly reminded the PR man that Yoko was Japanese, Cohen calmed down and spilled the tea. To maintain strict confidentiality, Yoko was organizing every detail. Apparently, John's overriding concern was maintaining total secrecy over the recording sessions until he was confident that the new record was going to work. After a few days in the studio, if John was not comfortable with the musicians, the songs, or that things were coming together, he could simply pull the plug and walk away. As long as nothing had leaked to the media, John's reputation would be preserved. Yoko had impressed upon Cohen that her number-one priority was to protect her husband from embarrassment in the media.

But this would be no easy feat in a media-saturated city like the Big Apple. "She says she doesn't trust any New York City freelance photographer," Cohen continued. "She's afraid they might take the photos and sell them to local papers." This seemed crazy to Farrington, who noted that "independent photographers like me own our images, and if we did that, we'd be violating our agreement of client first-usage. You could get sued for something like that!" Ignoring the photographer's bout of legalese, Cohen began speaking in the third-person, reminding him that Yoko's effort to maintain secrecy at all costs was why "she decided to look outside the city to find publicity agents and photographers she could trust, and looked to Boston, where an obvious first choice would be the boutique PR agency of Charles J. Cohen, with his successful track record of working with well-known entertainment celebrities and his extensive local and national media Rolodex."

Having taken Farrington fully into his confidence, Cohen explained the plan that Yoko had recently hatched. In preparation for the Lennons' return to public life, she had secretly booked a New York recording studio, the Hit Factory, and retained a music producer, Jack Douglas, whom John knew well and trusted. For his part, Douglas was to retain top studio musicians without telling any of them who they would be working with, or anything else about the record or studio, for that matter. John also wanted Yoko's music to be featured on the record, but they were still working those details out. They had settled on August 7 at high noon for John and Yoko to make the trip to the Hit Factory, where they would begin working with Douglas and the musicians.

"Plan A," as Cohen described it, was for Farrington to meet the Lennons at the Dakota and document the proceedings, recognizing full well that the local media would inevitably find out about John and Yoko's plans and crash the party. If this were to happen—either by mistake or, worse, an insider dropping a dime to *The New York Daily News*—an official photo could be put in play immediately in accordance with the end-of-day deadline. In turn, this would enable Yoko to justify a ban on

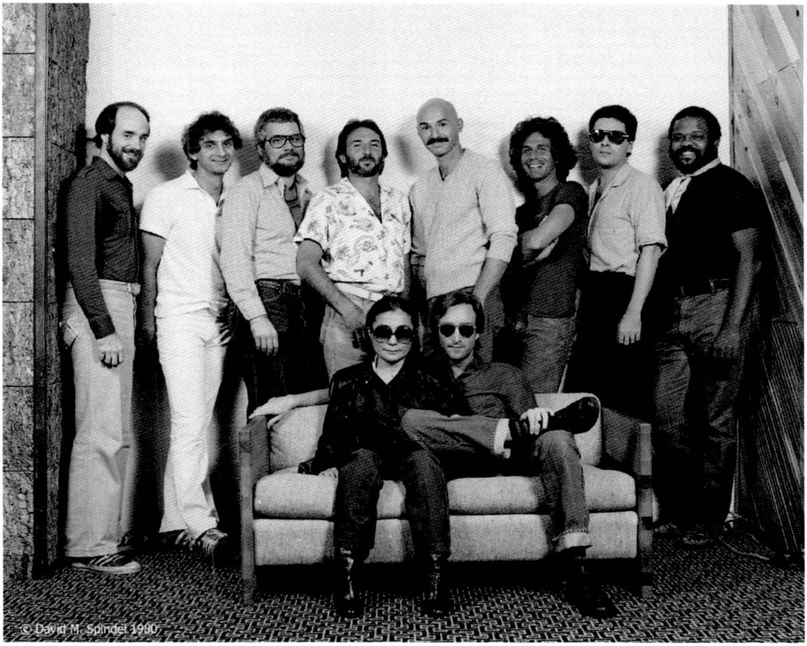

9. Yoko, John, and the *Double Fantasy* band, September 8, 1980; from left to right: George Small (keyboards), Jack Douglas (producer), Lee DeCarlo (engineer), Hugh McCracken (guitar), Tony Levin (bass), Andy Newmark (drums), Earl Slick (guitar), and Arthur Jenkins Jr. (percussion).

news photographers and reporters in the studio. As soon as the musicians and recording team gathered, Cohen surmised, there would be too many folks involved to prevent someone from spilling the beans about John and Yoko's presence at the Hit Factory. For her part, Yoko was concerned that John would lose his cool and pull the plug immediately. To avert any number of disastrous outcomes, Cohen figured that his best play would be to have Farrington prepare a photo for immediate distribution so that Yoko could maintain a semblance of control.

"Plan B," which seemed far-fetched given the New York City media's tenacity, would come into play if the "Big Secret" were somehow contained during the first few days of the sessions. In that scenario, Yoko would remain in control of the media announcement and deadline pressure would ease considerably. She and Cohen could hold Farrington's photo for a day or two and enjoy the luxury of having time to schedule media interviews and additional photo opportunities. All the while, John would be afforded sufficient time to find a nice groove with his band and gain confidence in his new songs.

But before anything could proceed, Cohen explained, Yoko needed to know Farrington's numbers—namely, when he was born. This was no idle request, he remarked. "John and Yoko have a team of astrologists, psychics, and fortune tellers on their payroll," said Cohen. "They are all on call twenty-four hours a day, seven days a week. Every important decision that John or Yoko makes goes through them first. Every person involved in the recording, including all the musicians, studio personnel, and even you, had to be vetted through her astrologist. Yoko had them do astrology charts on everyone." On the eve of the shoot, Cohen announced to Farrington that "you can tell your friends that you got the job because of your birthday. John Lennon's birthday is October 9th, and you're September 30th, so you both have the same sign, Libra, right?"

To Farrington's way of thinking, having his professional qualifications overridden by astrological analysis and numerological interpretation added yet another layer of uncertainty to this bizarre, top-secret assignment. But he knew implicitly that the only key for ensuring success under either of Cohen's scenarios had nothing to do with the whimsy of the stars. Farrington's job, above everything else, was to land the perfect shot.

As August 7 approached, Farrington's overarching concern had nothing to do with astrology. "Even after all of Cohen's instructions, I simply did not feel as professionally prepared as I should be. The dots were not connecting together in my mind," he recalled, "and I was not feeling the job flow naturally. There hadn't been any discussion yet about what 'the shot' was going to be. During a shoot, being prepared for what is going to happen next instills a degree of confidence in photographers for when those magical, one-of-a-kind moments occur. Not unlike a dance or theater performance, the photographer plays a supporting role with the other lead 'actors' in the scene—namely, the subjects—working together in lockstep, shot by shot."

But Yoko's haphazard approach—and by extension, Cohen's vagueness—was causing incredible anxiety for Farrington. The day before the shoot, the photographer and the PR flak huddled in Cohen's Boston office for last-minute preparations. "Just in case you're still wondering," he announced, "Yoko's hiring you to be the official first-day photographer. You will be reimbursed for your airfare and taxis—just put them on your invoice with everything else. In fact, Yoko wants you to bill my office for the entire job."

The gist of the meeting was clear: Cohen needed one usable black-and-white photograph to accompany the press release. Yet incredibly, at the eleventh hour, Cohen was still remaining vague about what exactly "the shot" itself should look like. To make matters worse, Farrington realized that he would be working on a remarkably tight schedule. "Calculating the day's hour-by-hour timeline—from driving to the airport, catching the 10:00 A.M. Logan shuttle, taxi rides to the Dakota, Hit Factory, and back to LaGuardia, then a rush-hour drive to the lab, where he would process the film and have prints by 6:00 P.M.—there was simply no room for any delay or screw-up." By his rudimentary calculations, at most he would have about an hour, possibly two, in John and Yoko's presence to get the perfect shot—*whatever that was*.

To Farrington's growing frustration, Cohen insisted on keeping things loose. Yoko and the PR man had concocted a media strategy in which Farrington would arrive at Studio One by noon, where he would meet Yoko and possibly John himself. Then he would be required to take a taxi over to the Dakota by himself, somehow gain entry to the studio, and hopefully shoot some pictures. Prior experience had taught him that no matter what happened—whether he missed the deadline or somehow missed the key shot (while changing film, or not being in the correct spot)—it would be entirely Farrington's fault.

And to make things even more complicated, Cohen added that "there are no guarantees that you will meet or photograph John or Yoko. There are no guarantees that you will meet them at the Dakota or even get into the recording studio with them. You may arrive at the Dakota and be told to go home. You may get into the Hit Factory and be kicked out. You may not tell anyone that you are with Yoko or working for the Lennons. Everything is still top secret until you're told otherwise. But don't worry, you will still be paid. Just remember, you are not officially with John and Yoko, and you are not to tell anyone that you are working for them, or even with them." In fact, Farrington wasn't even supposed to ride with the couple to the studio. "Yoko wants you to hail a cab and follow their limo to the Hit Factory." Stranger yet, "Yoko would like you to get to the Hit Factory ahead of them, if possible, and be hanging around nearby on the sidewalk, maybe half a block away. She wants you to make it look like you are a regular guy with a camera walking down the street and suddenly you recognize John Lennon and Yoko Ono and start snapping pictures. You follow them, taking more photos and discreetly tail them into the Hit Factory building and into the recording studio. But if anyone stops you, you absolutely cannot say, 'I'm with John and Yoko.' You're on your own and have to figure it out."

Cohen finally came to the issue of capturing the perfect shot to accompany the press release. "If you somehow get into the recording studio, you probably won't be able to shoot during the recording session, so try to get a few shots as quickly as you can and then head back to Boston." But what they really needed, Cohen emphasized, was "one usable photo of John and Yoko that shows them coming out of retirement, going back into the recording studio to start work on a new album. You'll just have to do your best and get what you can get. I know you can do it."

Before they adjourned, Cohen relayed a final question from his client: "Yoko wants to know who will own all the photographs." As an independent contractor, Farrington's position was rote. "I own all my images unless I transfer the copyrights and original negatives in writing and with further compensation," he replied. "This is standard Massachusetts and federal law for musicians, authors, and photographers," he reminded him. "If Yoko wants to own all the photos after the shoot, she will have to purchase the negatives in what's called a 'buyout,' and I will put the copyright transfer of each numbered photo in writing."

It suddenly dawned on Farrington that this shoot was a particularly unusual job in more ways than one. "Because Lennon is so famous, as for the valuation of negatives and copyrights for the buyout," he told Cohen, "we'd have to have the negatives and copyrights appraised as to their total present and future valuation." His discourse was met with a bored expression from Cohen, who was eager to get on with the next day's extraordinary events, whatever they turned out to be. Photo or no photo, it would all be over in twenty-four hours.

Not surprisingly, the whole business seemed absurd to Farrington. He realized that meeting the deadline within such strict conditions was going to be difficult under the best of circumstances. In those days, clients and agencies hired freelance photographers to develop and print negatives onto "contact sheets," which showcase the individual prints for the client's inspection and selection prior to publication. In those predigital times, all 35-mm film was manufactured with a series of numbers running alongside the film's perforated edges. The numbers appeared—1–1A, 2–2A, and 3–3A, up to 36A—on the film after development.

To create a contact sheet, a processed roll of thirty-six exposure film would be cut into six strips of six exposures each. These delicate strips of negatives had to be carefully handled and stored to prevent scratches, fingerprints, and dust, which would cause imperfections to appear on the final prints. The process would result in thirty-six tiny, numbered photographs on a single piece of photo paper. Contact sheets were the main currency between photographer and client for ordering the final 8 × 10 glossy prints. Often, publicity agencies like Cohen's would then schedule office meetings with their clients to make their selections. From what Farrington could ferret out, there was simply no instance in Yoko and Cohen's breakneck schedule that allowed for the usual process to take place.

On the night before the shoot, Farrington gathered up his gear. "I had learned from past experience that grabbing the camera bag on my way out the door was one sure way to forget something important, like extra batteries, a special lens, or enough film," he recalled. "After years of jobs, I had streamlined my camera bag down to fit my style and cover the majority of quick publicity jobs. It carried two Nikon FM camera bodies, one with auto winder attached; three Nikkor F2 and F2.8 lenses covering 28 mm (wide angle), 35 mm (less wide angle), and 105 mm (short telephoto) with lens shades; one fully charged Honeywell Strobonar with an extra battery (also charged), a camera mounting bracket for strobe, one- and two-stop light-diffusing strobe domes, strobe to camera shutter release sync cord, two extra sync cords; color, B&W and color slide films of various types and speeds; and assorted lens-cleaning tissue, Q-tips, sync cord tip conditioning tool, and extra strobe bulb." For the next day's shoot, he was especially concerned about the shifting light conditions between the Dakota and recording studio interiors and the sunny New York City streetscape. As for film, he used Kodak Tri-X 400 speed film for indoor situations under ambient light, Kodak Plus-X 125 two-stop, slower speed film for outdoor sunlight.

As the shuttle left Logan Airport for New York City, Farrington arrived at a moment of clarity that snapped him out of nearly a month's worth of mental doubt and insecurity. "To make this shoot work, I had to completely block out who my famous subjects were and view John and Yoko as ordinary people. Their past antics didn't matter." He psyched himself up by realizing that "my assignment today is to capture John and Yoko as a creative duo for a new decade and with a new sound. It didn't matter what they looked like; my shots will be clear and sharp, showing facial details not seen in years. I will be witness to a new chapter in music history being written today. If this is the ultimate photo assignment, I will be ready."

Pulling up outside of the Dakota, Farrington reasoned that in many ways the day's photo session, with its candid nature, its question marks

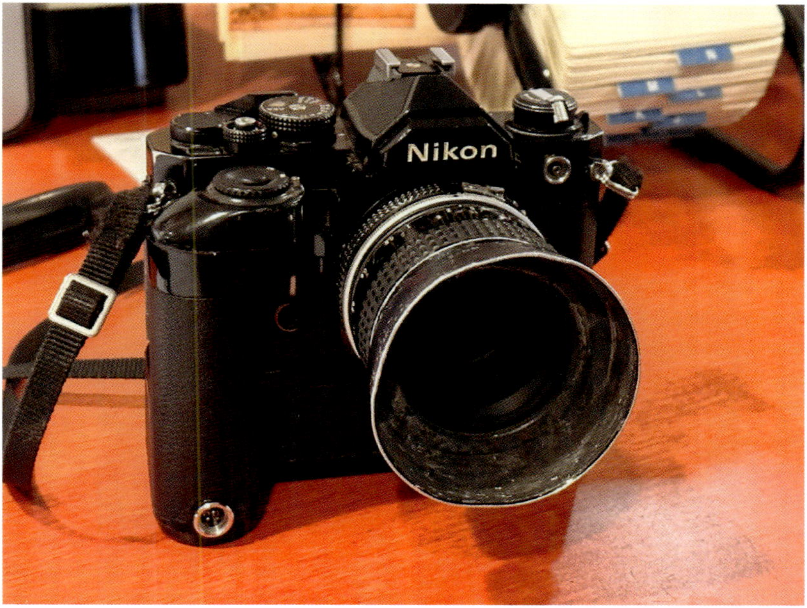

10. Nikon FM camera.

and uncertainties, would be like covering a wedding. “Once a wedding starts, it is like a train leaving the station,” said Farrington. “It stops for no one, including inexperienced photographers who might be stuck loading film while the bouquet is flying over their heads. Candid photographers only have one chance to get most key shots, and when they do, they get more jobs. Having incorporated my prior wedding skills into my commercial publicity business had paid off tremendously. Advance preparation was the best way to serve wedding and publicity clients for capturing ‘candid,’ real-life-looking shots. It is ironic but true that those planned-in-advance ‘candid’ moments yielded the best publicity photographs. I’ve heard it said that candid photography involves a conspiracy between subject and photographer.”

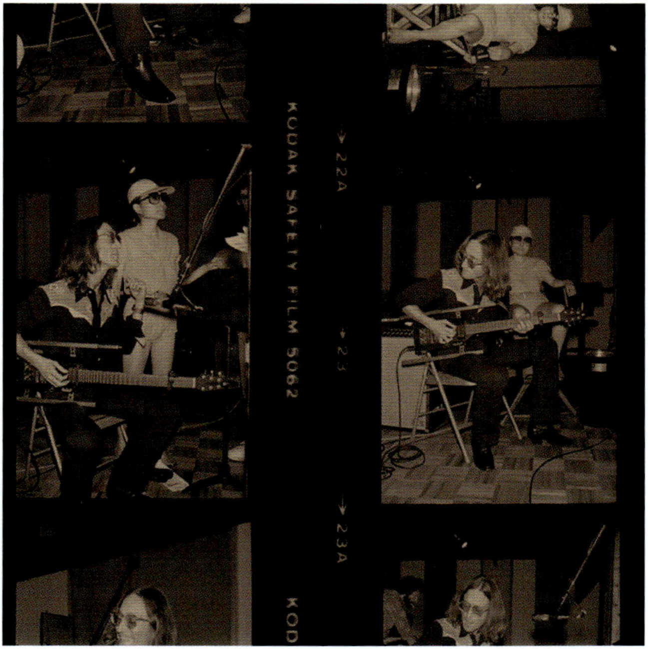
KODAK SAFETY FILM 5062
22A
23
23A

4.

The Dakota

The extraordinary nature of Farrington's assignment hit home when he asked the Yellow Cab driver at LaGuardia to take him to One West 72nd Street. "That's the Dakota apartments, right? That's quite a place," said the cabbie. "Lots of celebrities live there." To provide a little misdirection for his top-secret mission, Farrington replied, "Doesn't Leonard Bernstein live there?" And that's when his cab driver, a proud New Yorker, said, "That's where John Lennon lives—you know, from the Beatles?" Farrington could see the man beaming in the rearview mirror. "I wish he'd put the Beatles back together again," the cabbie added, "but I guess he needed a break."

When he arrived at the august Upper West Side address, an 85°F heat welcomed Farrington to the Dakota. Gazing up at the dark, Gothic edifice, he stepped out of the cab, fully clad with a necktie and a tan summer suit. Lugging his camera bag on his shoulder, he was welcomed by a uniformed doorman, who directed him to the building's porte cochere, and, just beyond, the reception desk. Before going inside, he noticed that the streetscape was relatively quiet—void of any other photographers, media types, or autograph seekers. Given the sunny, midday conditions, "I realized that photographing the Lennons as they exited from a shadowy passageway onto a bright sidewalk was going to necessitate a series of extreme camera adjustments while walking backwards. Moments later, as he waited for the receptionist to direct him to Studio One, Farrington caught a glimpse of the daily mail, which included an envelope addressed to "Ms. Betty Bacall." Lauren Bacall. A true Hollywood legend of the golden age. Farrington certainly wasn't in Boston anymore.

By the time he reached Studio One, Farrington was ready to get to work. But his efforts would be delayed, if only for the moment, by the pressing matter of a hat. When he first entered the room, he observed an air of tension, which he chalked up to the importance of the day. As he watched, Yoko's assistants carried on a hushed conversation about the missing accessory. Apparently, Yoko had ordered a hat from a local boutique, and the messenger service had not delivered it yet. From what Farrington could ascertain, the missing yellow baseball cap was a top priority. But just as suddenly, the crisis had been averted. The ball cap would be arriving shortly by cab. As he wondered about how to proceed with the photo session, Yoko abruptly emerged from her inner sanctum. "As our eyes met," Farrington recalled, "I stood up and walked over to greet her. Yoko looked great, wearing a turquoise hot-pants jumpsuit that complemented her well-toned legs."

"Nice to meet you, Mrs. Lennon," the photographer cheerfully announced, extending his hand in greeting. But to his embarrassment, Farrington was met with a blank silence. Had he already blown his once-in-a-lifetime opportunity? "Maybe I had offended her somehow," he thought. "Perhaps her first impression was off—was it my necktie?" He began to wonder if the job had already been canceled, and she would be sending him back to Boston. Suddenly, he wished that Cohen had been there to help break the ice. But then Yoko took his hand, softly shook it, and asked, "You are coming over to the studio with us? Are you staying over tonight and going back to the studio with us again tomorrow?"

Suddenly, Farrington was more confused than ever. Wasn't it her explicit instruction that he return to Boston that same day to process the film? "Well, no, um, I'm only here today," he replied awkwardly, "to get a good shot as soon as possible and fly back to Boston."

In his mind, Farrington was cursing Cohen to no end. "Did I actually just turn down an invitation to be an overnight guest of the Lennons?" But just as quickly, the moment had passed. "John will be down in a few minutes and then we'll be going to the studio," she replied. What Yoko had suggested made perfect sense. A two-day assignment, rather than a same-day pressurized rush job, was the obvious solution. No pressure, get to know the clients, find a comfort zone, have some fun, and get great shots. Had Cohen devised the breakneck schedule to maintain total control over the shoot?

That was Farrington's cue. As he waited outside Yoko's office, he readied his equipment. "It was almost time," he recalled. "I quickly unzipped my camera bag and pulled out my Nikon FM with winder attached and 35-mm lens. I checked the viewfinder, confirmed the frame counter read '1,' and back-tensioned the film rewind gear to confirm the film was loaded correctly." After attaching the camera's strobe unit, he double-checked his equipment to ensure that it was in working order. Minutes later, the door flew open to reveal Fred Seaman, John and Yoko's assistant. With long, shaggy sandy hair, and a newly tanned complexion, he was dressed in faded old blue jeans and a white T-shirt. "You're the photographer!" he said. "Nice to meet you. I'll be driving you over to the Hit Factory in a few minutes," he instructed, suddenly putting to rest Farrington's anxiety. "I'll be in John's Mercedes four-door," he quickly added. "I'll pull up out front behind the limo. After you've taken your photos, just jump in."

And that's when John finally made the scene. Farrington recalled hearing the musician's voice before actually seeing him in the flesh. "I could hear John singing," he remembered. "The sound seemed to resonate through the office door and behind the rows of file cabinets—as if he was singing his way down a back stairway before entering the office. It was an unmistakable voice that I had heard thousands of times before." Farrington was taken aback as Lennon strode into the room: "He was taller than I expected and dressed head to toe in black Western-style garb. He looked thin, fit, and freshly tanned like Fred, and with long locks of light brown hair flowing around his shoulders beneath a huge wide-brimmed black hat. He looked every inch the famous rock star that indeed he was. It was an impressive entrance, beyond all my expectations."

In contrast with Yoko's air of tension, John's demeanor was characterized by a bright-eyed enthusiasm. He was energized, ready to go, and today was obviously the day. His buoyant mood matched the colorfully patterned, red-and-white shoulder yoke that he wore, an ensemble that was completed by a pair of black cowboy boots, pants, and shirt. As with Fred, John greeted Farrington warmly. "Looking up into his eyes, I was awestruck," Farrington admitted. "That voice continued speaking to me. 'I'm John Lennon,' he said with a nod. 'Nice to meet you. So you're the photographer, are you? Well, I thought you were one of the accountants!'" For his part, Farrington could barely speak. "With no witty reply to John's good-natured banter, I managed a nodding laugh and barely managed a reply: 'Ah, well no, I'm here to get a couple of photos.'"

As John busied himself with Yoko's assistants, his wife joined them in the outer office. "Don't speak to him," she told Farrington. Suddenly, she was all business. "You're not to speak to John," she clarified in a voice that was loud enough for everyone to hear, including her husband. Farrington was aghast. "What hit me the hardest was Yoko seemed angry," he recalled. "Her remarks were disappointing and unexpected, certainly in light of our recent conversation. What on earth had I possibly done wrong to deserve this rebuke from Yoko?" Farrington reconsidered his earlier conclusion about Cohen's duplicity. Perhaps Yoko had been confusing Cohen these past few weeks with too many conflicting instructions? Whatever the reason, Farrington returned to his mission. "I could not dwell on these thoughts," he realized. "I had a job to do. *No talking to John*. Got it."

While he gave his camera equipment a final check, John and Yoko briefly retreated into the inner office. When they reemerged moments later, John was carrying a slim attaché case, while Yoko was wearing a bright yellow baseball cap. Apparently, the tardy accessory had finally arrived. As the couple headed toward the door, John remarked, "Come on, dearie. It's time to get going." Glancing at Farrington, he continued, "Mr. Photographer, do what you gotta do!" Seeing his chance, Farrington whispered to John, "I just need a shot of the two of you together." Making eye contact, the former Beatle nodded in his direction. Taking his cue, Farrington slipped in front of the couple so that he could capture them leaving the Dakota together. "And then I was out the door," the photographer recalled. "With a little adrenaline flowing, I quickly passed the front desk, pushed open the side door, went down the steps, and exited the courtyard towards the street." Turning around and staring through his lens, Farrington was treated to a rather dimly lit scene. As John and Yoko entered the porte cochere, he activated his strobe and prepared to capture the first photo of the Lennons leaving the Dakota on this historic day.

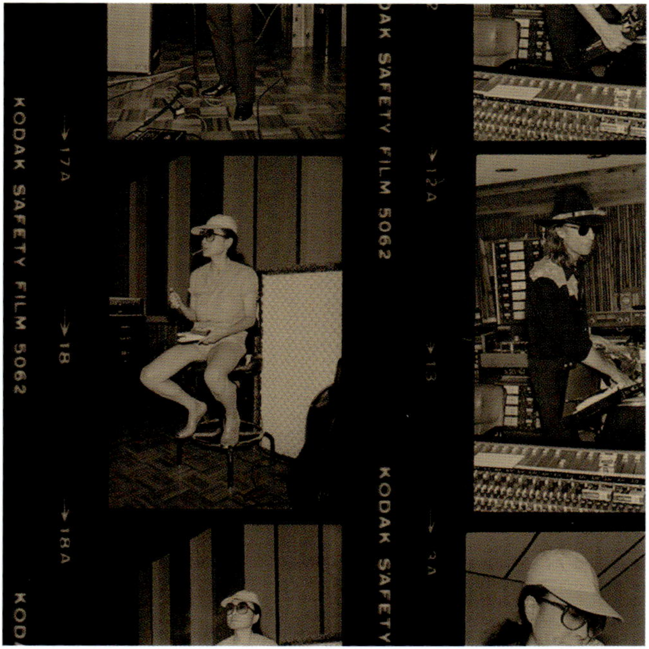

5.

West 72nd

As events unfolded on that fateful afternoon, Farrington quickly learned that establishing a rapport with his famous subjects, especially Yoko, would be the key to any hope for a successful shoot. As they exited the porte cochere, it became abundantly clear that John was old hat when it came to photo sessions. He knew the drill, while his wife was understandably less sure of herself in such situations. And then there was the matter of her gnawing anxiety. If nothing else, Cohen had certainly been right about Yoko's overriding concern. For her part, Yoko seemed positively nervous—far more nervous than Farrington even, with his strange assignment—that something might go wrong right there outside the Dakota and catapult John back into the sanctity of the Dakota. Outside on the streetscape, with the midday sunlight fully in evidence, Farrington could make out light-colored food stains on Yoko outfit, a strange occurrence for a woman who had seemed so pulled together, so tautly arrayed in terms of her clothing and demeanor over the years. To Farrington's mind, there was no doubt about it: She had been concerned for her husband all along.

As they made their way onto the sidewalk that fronted West 72nd Street, Farrington continued jockeying for position in front of the couple so that he could document the occasion. Somehow, Yoko had managed to move several steps in front of her husband. "Instead of backpedaling as she approached me," said Farrington, "I held my ground to hopefully slow her down. Just as she was filling the frame in my viewfinder, John immediately recognized what was happening. 'Mother dear,' he called out while reaching forward to grab her arm from behind, 'slow down. We're doing this together.' In the exact moment that his hand touched her arm, I made the first exposure."

Farrington knew that the first shot wouldn't be *the one*, that it wasn't a winner. As John and Yoko entered the porte cochere, Farrington backpedaled around a parked car, lining up his next shot in the driveway as the couple stepped off the sidewalk, their hands now tightly locked together. "As I carefully focused the camera, I felt a gust of wind on my back and saw John's hair puff out under his hat's wide brim. I took the shot and felt it was a good one."

John looked great. They both looked great—Yoko's food stains notwithstanding—wearing cool outfits and sunglasses, their expressions serious and determined. "Wow," Farrington thought to himself in relief, "I have one good shot."

Glancing at his wristwatch, Farrington realized that it was already 1:00 P.M. The quiet streetscape that had greeted him an hour earlier seemed to have filled with bystanders in the interim. As the Lennons stepped into the sunlight, Farrington took a few seconds to make quick F-stop adjustments for his next shot, while keeping an eye on his subjects and doing his level best not to trip over the curb while walking backward. "But just as I was bringing up the camera to my face," Farrington recalled, "I heard people on the sidewalk. A woman's voice called out, 'Is that John and Yoko?' while another offered, 'Hey, that's John Lennon. Hi, John!'" Farrington's worst fears seemed to be coming to fruition. "Oh my God," he thought, "the secret's already leaked out—they're probably reporters and photographers." Sensing the crowd moving closer, he quickly lined up his third shot as John and Yoko inched closer. "Just as I was tweaking

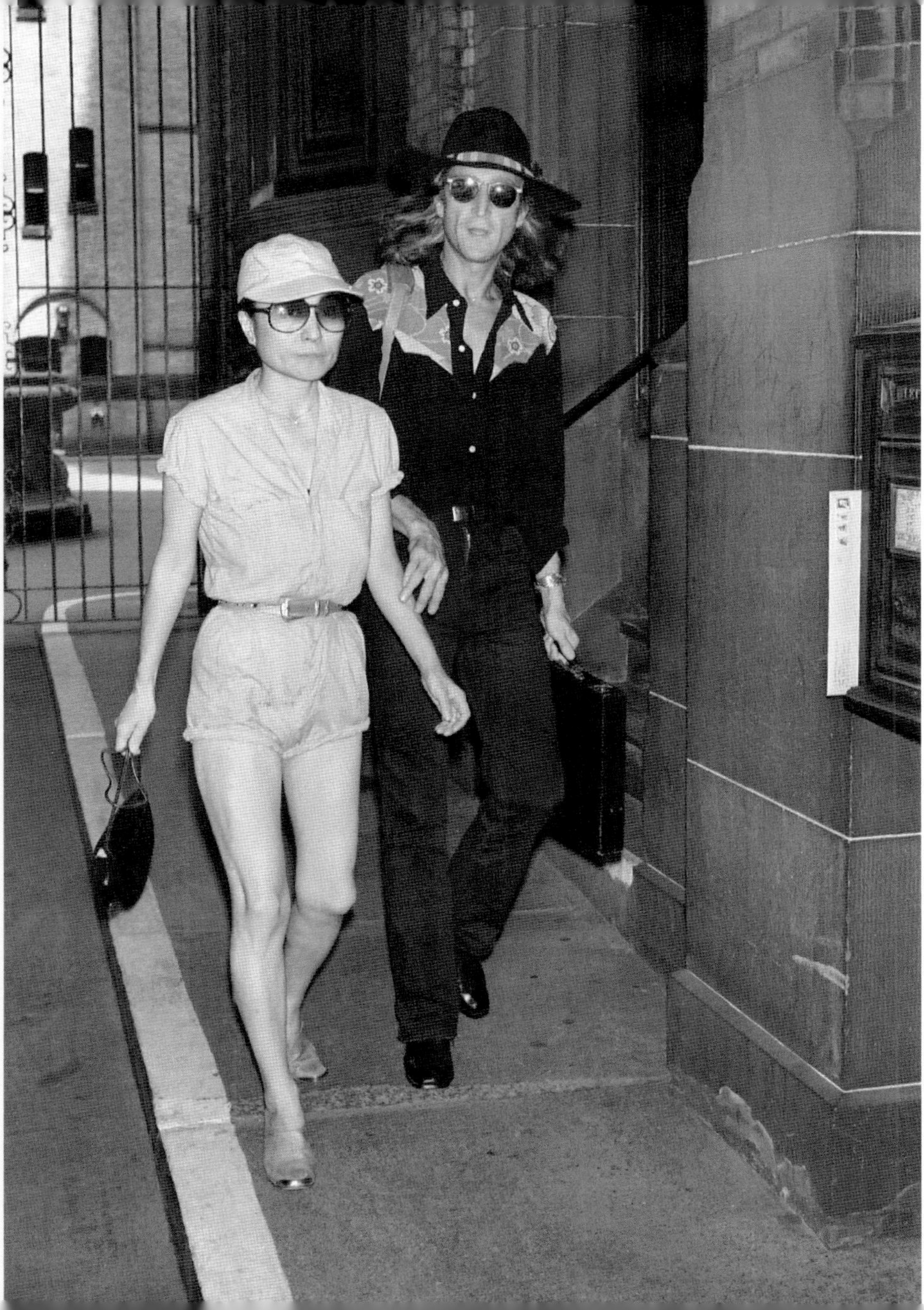

11. John and Yoko photo 1, August 7, 1980.

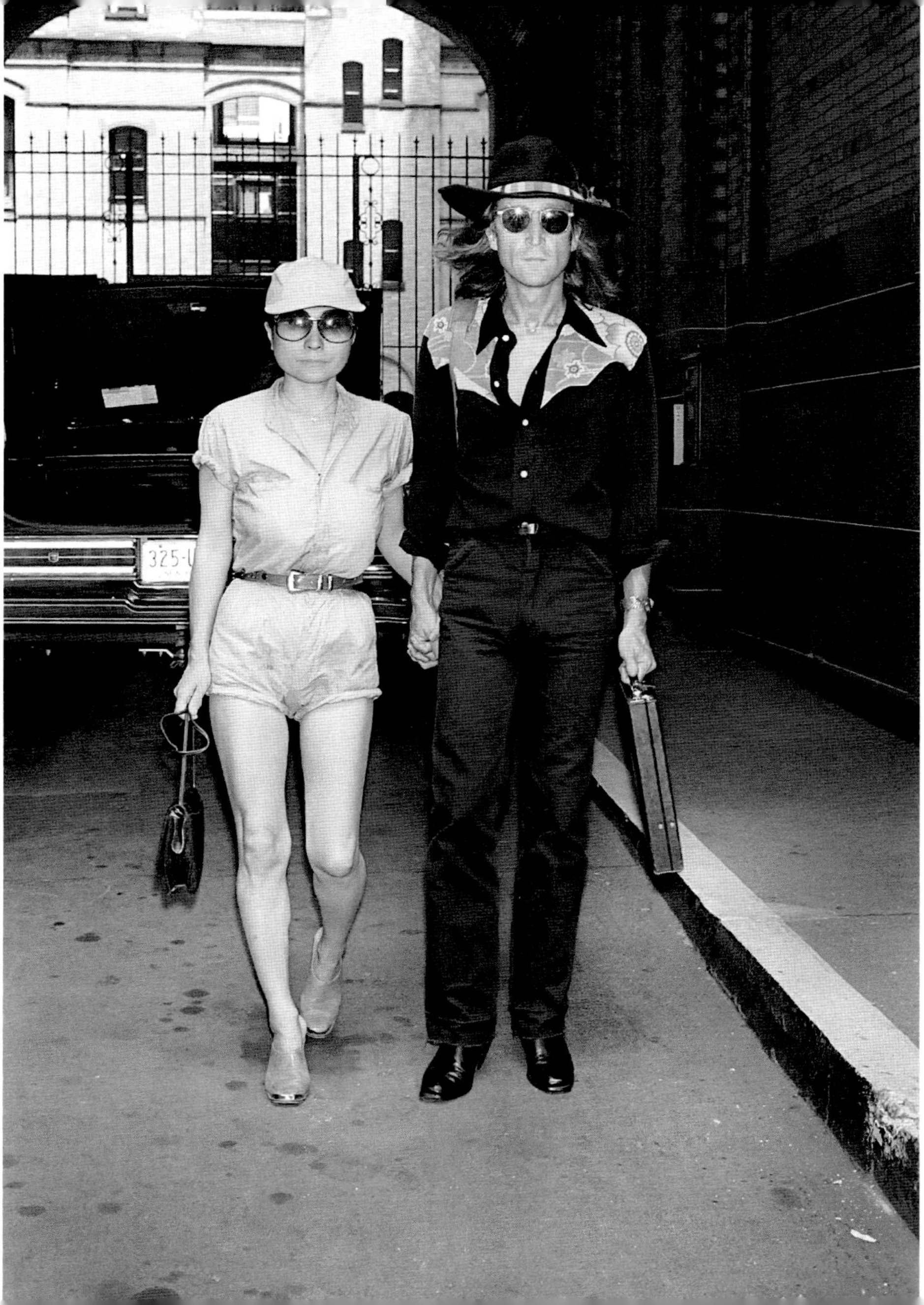

12. John and Yoko photo 2, August 7, 1980.

the focus and setting the strobe power to medium," said Farrington, "a loud male voice directly behind me shouted, 'Hey, John. Over here. Good luck today!" Recognizing the voice, John turned toward the man in the same instant that Farrington took the shot.

Farrington didn't know it at the time, but the man was twenty-one-year-old Paul Goresh, an amateur photographer whom John had alerted to the occasion. "Damn," Farrington whispered to himself, "that guy just ruined my shot! Who is that guy? Is he a press photographer?" In truth, Lennon and Goresh had a complicated history. Back in February 1979, Goresh had talked his way into the building—and ultimately into John and Yoko's apartment—by pretending to be a television repairman. He managed to get Lennon to sign his copy of *In His Own Write*, John's 1964 collection of witticisms. Within the month, Goresh began shadowing John as he strolled on the Upper West Side. This time, John was furious, clearly recognizing Goresh from his earlier visit to the Dakota. "I signed your book," Lennon exclaimed. "Don't take my photo. Leave me alone."[1]

At this point, Goresh decided that his mission to take John's picture would be better served through stealth. "I could get a telephoto lens, stand across the street from him, follow him, take a few pictures of him, and he'll never be any the wiser," Goresh reasoned. But his plan quickly imploded after John caught on to his ruse, brusquely removing the film from his camera and marching toward the safety of the Dakota archway. Now Goresh was truly despondent, having succeeded in sending his hero away in an angry huff. Leaving his Minolta behind, Goresh caught up with Lennon on the streets of the Upper West Side one more time. "I never meant to cause you grief," he told John. "If you want me to leave you alone, then I'll never come back here again." As they stood together on Central Park West, Goresh could sense Lennon beginning to let down his guard. "I remember he looked right in my eyes and said, 'Stop looking at me as a Beatle. You've got to treat me like you'd treat anyone else.' And he said, 'Come on,' and we went for a walk." Quite suddenly, Goresh was living out the fantasy of Beatles fans the world over, regularly

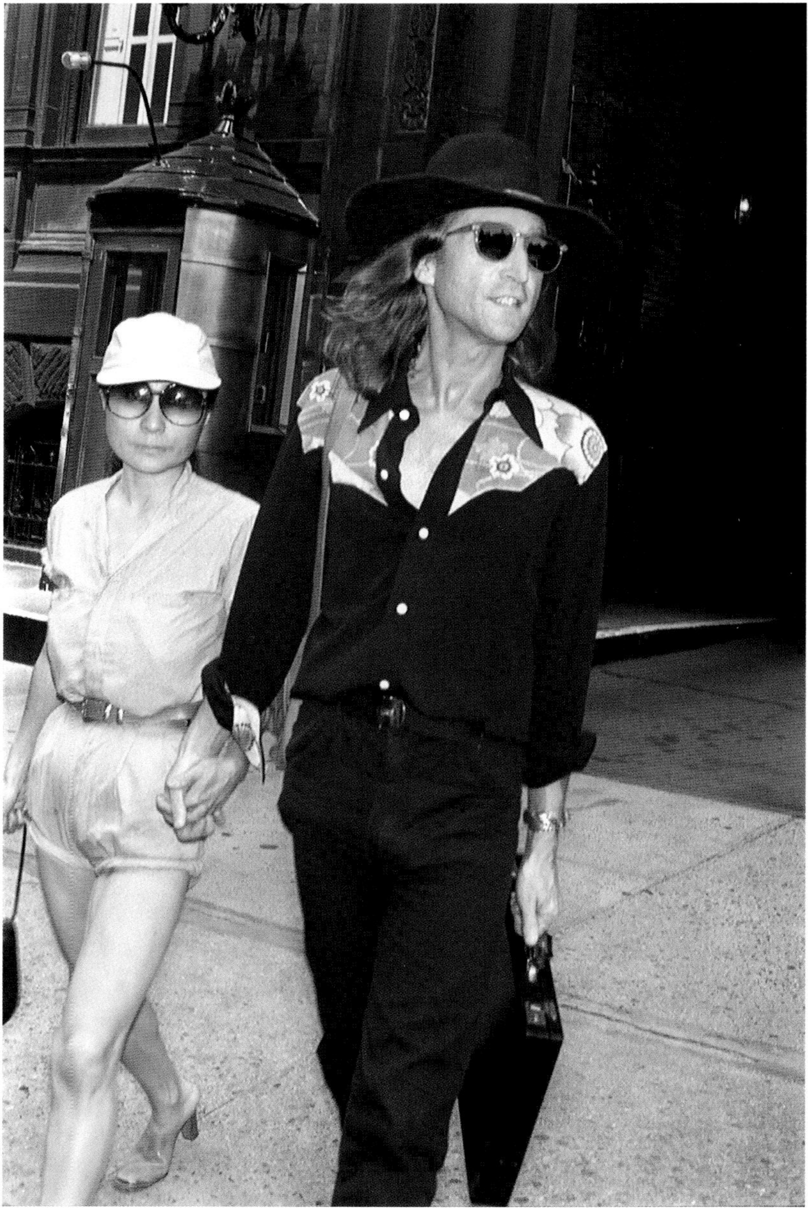

13. John and Yoko photo 3, August 7, 1980.

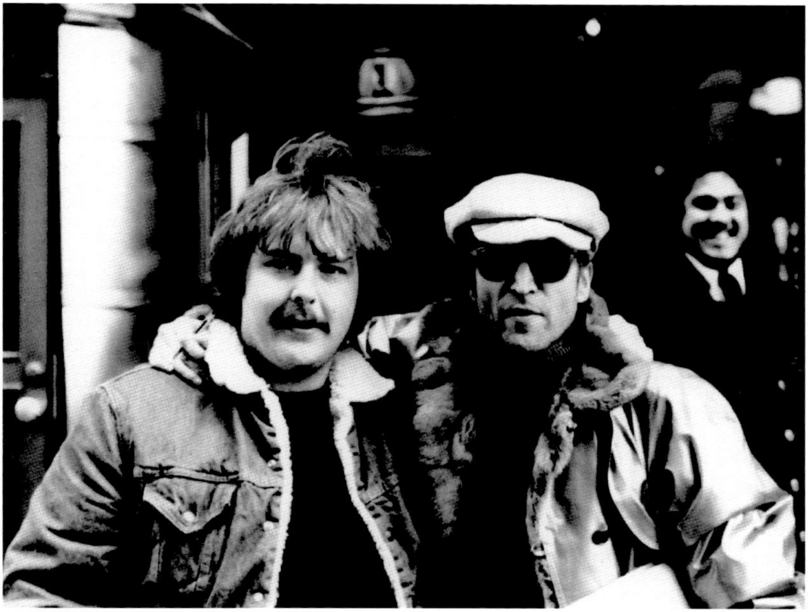

14. John Lennon and Paul Goresh, November 17, 1980.

accompanying John as he ran errands on the Upper West Side, tagging along as he strolled through Central Park.[2]

It would be nearly thirty years before Farrington learned the truth about Goresh's presence on West 72nd Street that day. As Farrington stood there on the sidewalk in front of the Dakota, Farrington was naturally concerned about Goresh's motives. For all he knew, the portly photographer might have been one of the aggressive types so prevalent during those predigital days when disorganized media "scrums" ruled the roost in photojournalism. "Before social media, when print journalism was king," said Farrington, "being a staff photographer for a big city daily was a highly coveted, well-paying job with many perks. Photo departments, not unlike sports teams, had a variety of key players with individual skill sets. Newspaper photo desks employed at least one tough photographer for those 'special' assignments where competition for prize-winning shots called for highly specialized skills. Editors treated them like princes." With the advent of digital photography, this tough-guy approach has become less significant. Today's photographers can view the images almost in the same moment in which they shoot them. Known for the practice of "chimping"—as in acting like a chimpanzee—digital photographers can easily exit the scrum, step back from the action, and scroll through their images to see if they've managed to get "the shot."

As it turned out, any concerns that Farrington had about Goresh had been for naught. He was a genuine amateur all right. In 2010, the two photographers spoke via telephone and reminisced about the historic day that the Lennons made their way to the Hit Factory for the first time. "I was out front when you were walking backwards taking pictures of John and Yoko as they were just coming out," Goresh told him. "I actually have a photo of you photographing John and Yoko." On August 6, Lennon had run into Goresh outside of the Dakota and announced that "tomorrow's going to be a big day, and we've hired a professional photographer. He'll be taking photos of Yoko and me leaving the Dakota and getting in the limo." John added that "I want you to leave him alone and stay out of his way." But at the same time, Goresh knew that John had given him the scoop of a lifetime, so when he made his way into the city that day, he carried his trusty Minolta XG1. When the Lennons stepped out of the Dakota that afternoon, Goresh managed to capture a shot of the couple exiting the archway, with John's eyes fixed squarely on the portly photographer.

Meanwhile, as John and Yoko approached the limousine that had been idling beside the curb, Farrington marveled at the lack of security in front of the Dakota. "Even a small crowd wanting photos or autographs can quickly grow larger and unruly, making it hard for 'trapped' celebrities to extricate themselves without assistance," said Farrington. "With a total lack of crowd control—police, public relations handlers, or private

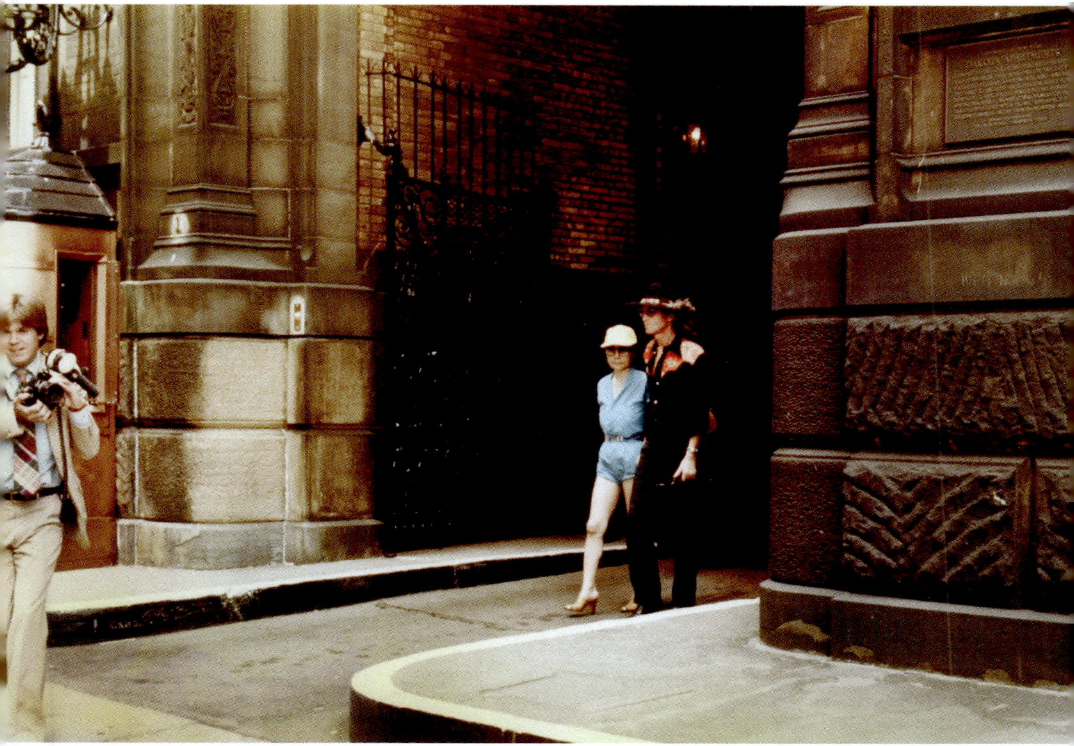

15. Goresh photo of Farrington, August 7, 1980.

security—it can be a roll of the dice. All it takes is an overly aggressive fan or an elbow-wielding, nasty press photographer to cause problems." As Farrington steadied his viewfinder, a voice from the crowd remarked, "Love your hat, John." As the former Beatle turned his head to acknowledge the compliment, Farrington took another shot.

Moments later, with John and Yoko safely ensconced inside the limo, the photographer managed to capture the image of Lennon waving to the crowd through his rolled-up window.

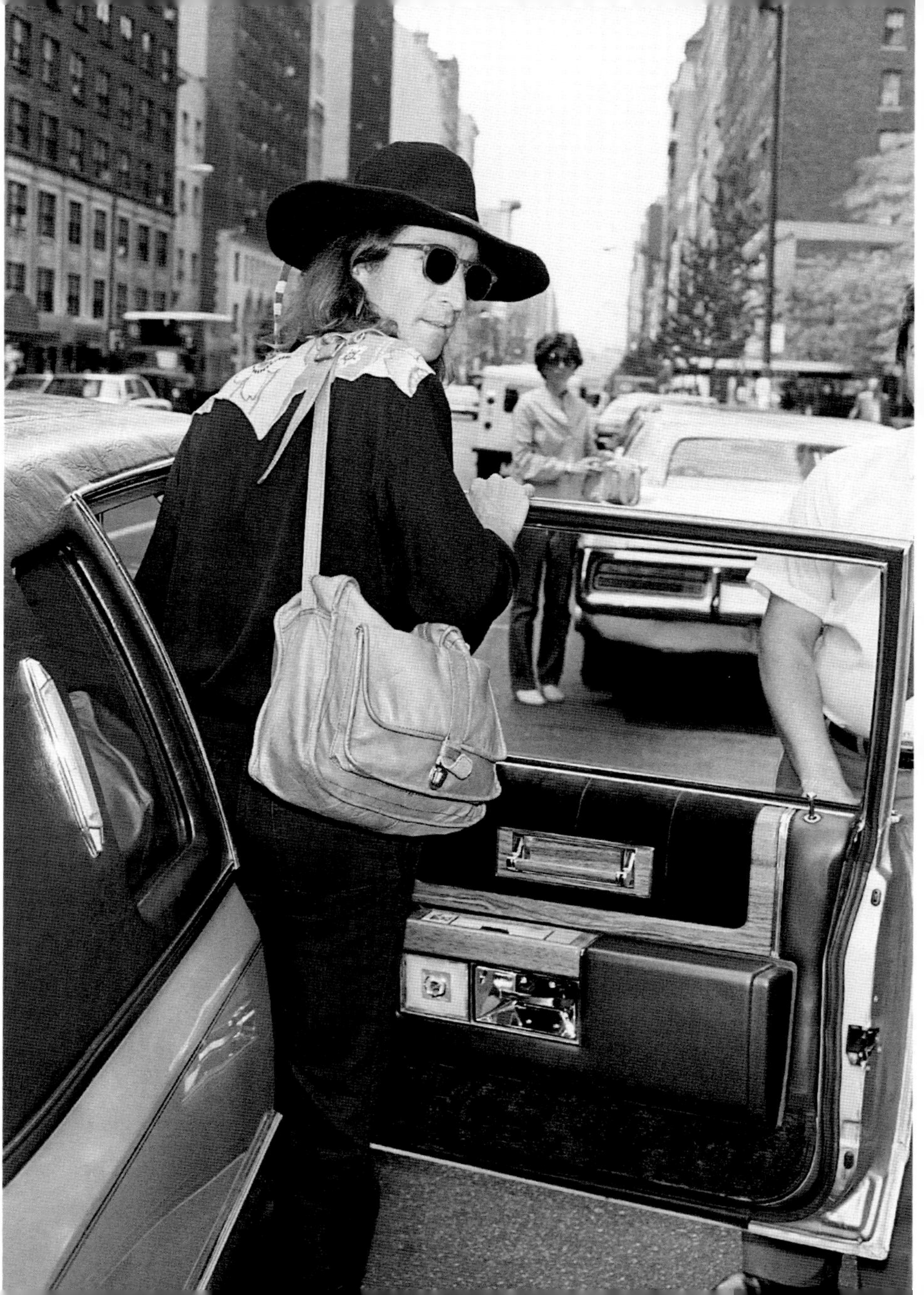

16. John and Yoko photo 4, August 7, 1980.

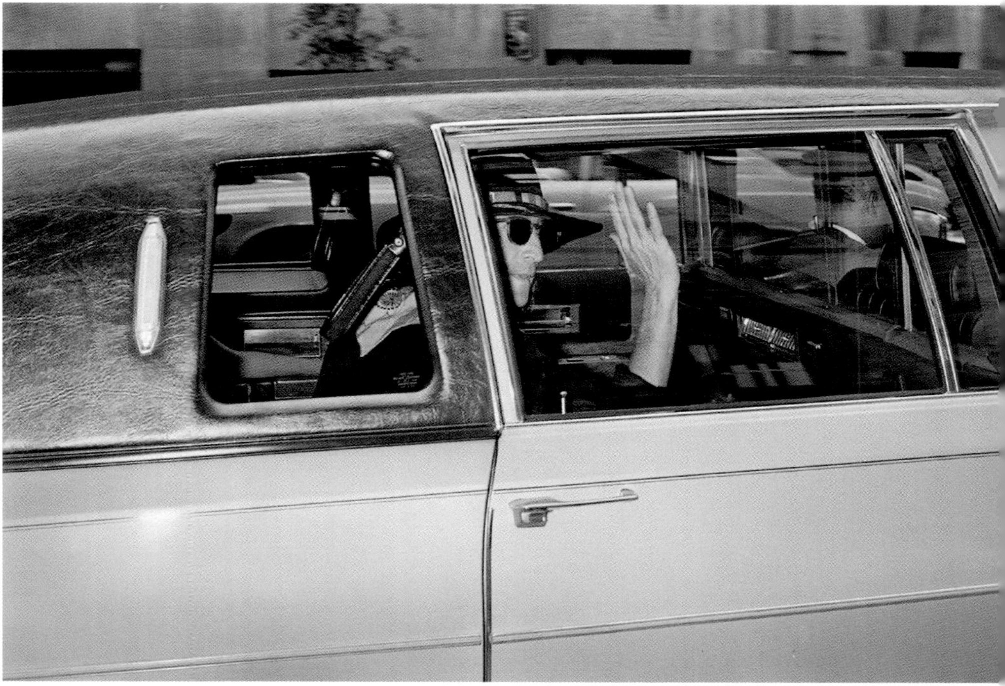

17. John and Yoko photo 5, August 7, 1980.

As Farrington observed the limo making its way down the street toward Columbus Avenue, Fred pulled up, as promised, in the Lennons' Mercedes-Benz station wagon. "Jump in!" Fred shouted. The photographer took notice of the guitar cases stacked up in the back seat. "You really have the best job in the world, Fred!" said Farrington, unable to contain his amazement. With the car's luxuriant air-conditioning washing over him in the passenger's seat, he removed his tie and stuffed it into his jacket pocket. After experiencing the melee in front of the Dakota, Farrington knew that the time for formality had once and truly passed.

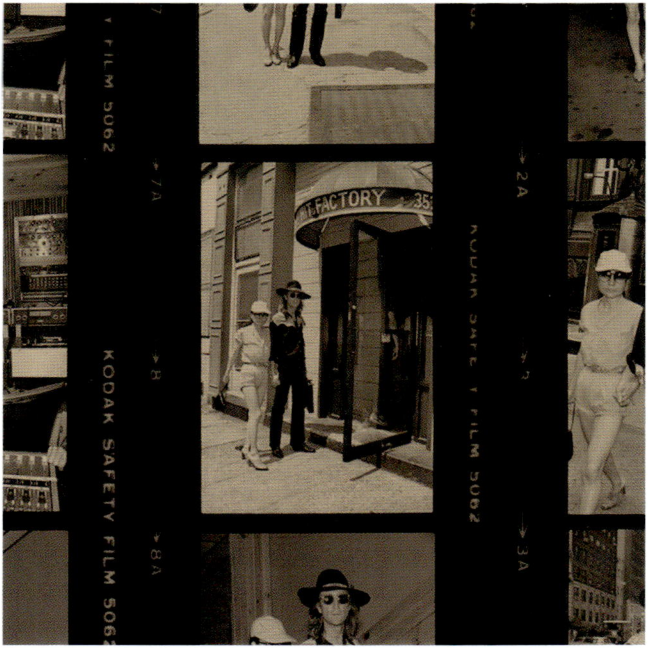

FILM 5062
7A
KODAK SAFETY FILM 5062
8
8A
FACTORY
2A
FILM 5062
3A

6.

Hit Factory

Almost as soon as they had pulled away from the Dakota, Fred and Farrington found themselves in heavy traffic thanks to a bridge accident. Worse yet, the limo was no longer in sight. The photographer understandably began to fret. "I really need to get to the Hit Factory before they do so I can line up arrival shots." But Fred seemingly had that aspect of their journey covered. "I'll get ahead and drop you off," he told him, "then park and bring the guitars up to the studio." That meant that when they arrived at the Hit Factory, Farrington would be on his own once again. "What if there was a crowd of pushy press photographers waiting in front of the Hit Factory?" he wondered. "Would I be able to slip past them into the studio without Fred's help?"

In the interim, Fred had managed to best the traffic and snake his way to the Hit Factory ahead of John and Yoko's limo. "Here we are!" he announced as they turned the corner onto West 48th. The wide street was completely empty, treeless, and entirely free of automobile and pedestrian traffic. Back in those days, gentrification hadn't crept into the far reaches of Hell's Kitchen. "Wow," Farrington exclaimed, "there's nobody here."

To his mind, it didn't feel like New York City anymore, a stark contrast from his experience outside of the Dakota, which was a mere twenty blocks or so to the north. With the hot city air breathing on his face, Farrington stared at the bland-looking office building that served as the Hit Factory's home. Farrington could see why Yoko had selected the Hit Factory instead of, say, more elite New York City studios like the Record Plant, the Power Station, or Electric Lady. It was way off the beaten track. The location certainly wasn't lost on producer Jack Douglas, who recalled that the Hit Factory was "in a building that no one would think to camp out in front of. No one would know. We could go in and out of there without ever being seen."[1]

And that's when Farrington caught sight of the building's faded semicircle awning, torn and blighted by pigeon droppings, lording over a nondescript entryway. Clearly printed on the awning were the words "353 THE HIT FACTORY 353." Farrington could see the makings of his perfect shot beginning to emerge before him. The image of John and Yoko casually walking underneath the studio entrance would make for a defining photograph to document the day. "That just might be THE shot," he thought to himself as he climbed out of the Mercedes and onto the vacant avenue. Moments later, the Lennons' limo pulled up on West 48th Street. The key to landing the perfect shot, Farrington reasoned, would be ensuring that he photographed the couple together. "As I approached the limo, positioning myself in a good angle and distance, I noticed the limo had parked in front of a partially bent-over, rusty old street sign," Farrington lamented. "Lining-up the shot through my viewfinder, it appeared in the middle of my composition, ruining any possible shot."

As Farrington stood there waiting for the Lennons to make their way toward the awning, he observed Yoko briskly exiting the limo, her pocketbook in hand, while John collected himself and stepped out of the car. "Wow," Farrington thought to himself, "he looks so cool in his black outfit arrayed against the bright sun." The bent signpost be damned. Farrington took the shot anyway with his strobe set to medium power.

He captured John in mid-speech as he reminded his wife, "Mother dear, hold up. We're doing this together." As with the scene back at the

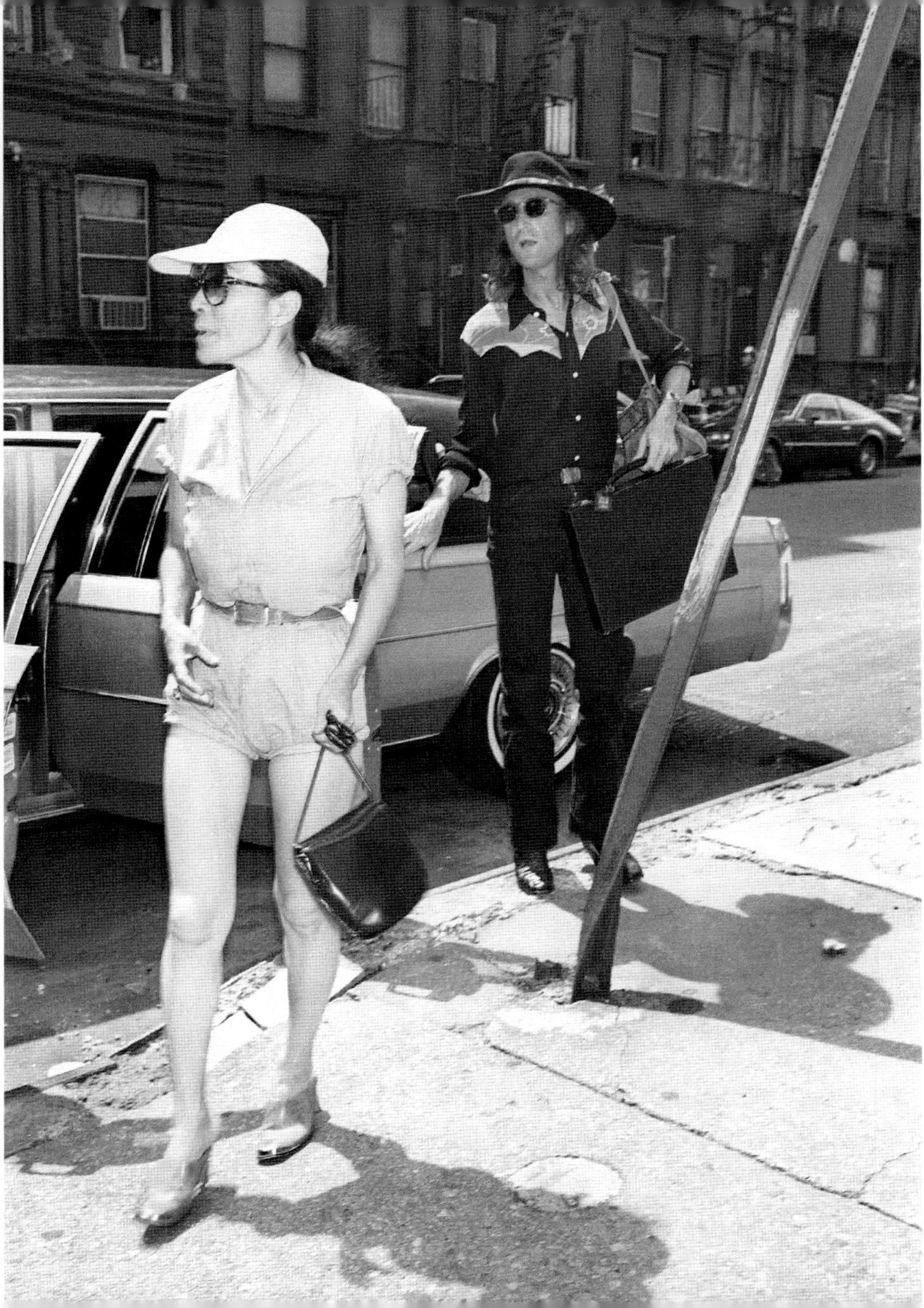

18. John and Yoko photo 6, August 7, 1980.

Dakota, Yoko seemed anxious, leaving her husband in her wake as she scanned the streetscape for any warning signs.

Slowly backpedaling along the deserted street, Farrington observed John as he caught up with Yoko and took her hand, their fingers clenched tightly together. The photographer thought back to Cohen's instructions—"She wants you to make it look like you are a regular guy with a camera walking down the street and suddenly you recognize John Lennon and Yoko Ono and start snapping pictures." This was surely the moment. It may have sounded ridiculous to Farrington a few weeks back, but suddenly he was transforming Cohen's vision into reality. As the limo pulled away, John and Yoko took his cue, standing together hand in hand on the sidewalk below the Hit Factory's facade. "You both look amazing," said Farrington as he focused the viewfinder. "Let's get a quick shot right here on the sidewalk before we go in. This looks great." Even in that instant, he could tell that the vertical shot held an iconic quality.

There they were, completely alone on a deserted sidewalk in New York City—John and Yoko, starting over, going back into the public eye. The cool hats, the hot pants, the briefcase—Farrington was pleased with his portraiture. In that light, even the rusty sign bending over the background frame seemed to lend an old-world effect to the image.

As the couple continued making their way along West 48th Street, Farrington positioned himself just beyond the studio entrance. For the first time that afternoon, the photographer felt that he and the Lennons were finally in sync, that they were working together toward a common goal. The next shot, which he had already titled in his mind's eye as "Entering the Hit Factory," would be crucial to say the least. He knew that his timing had to be perfect. As he framed the well-worn, semicircular Hit Factory awning with his viewfinder, he turned his strobe power to high. In the early afternoon sun, with both subjects wearing wide-brimmed hats, he knew that he had to blast some "fill" light onto their faces beyond what was already reflecting off the sidewalk. Without any additional strobe lighting, Farrington feared that it would be difficult to

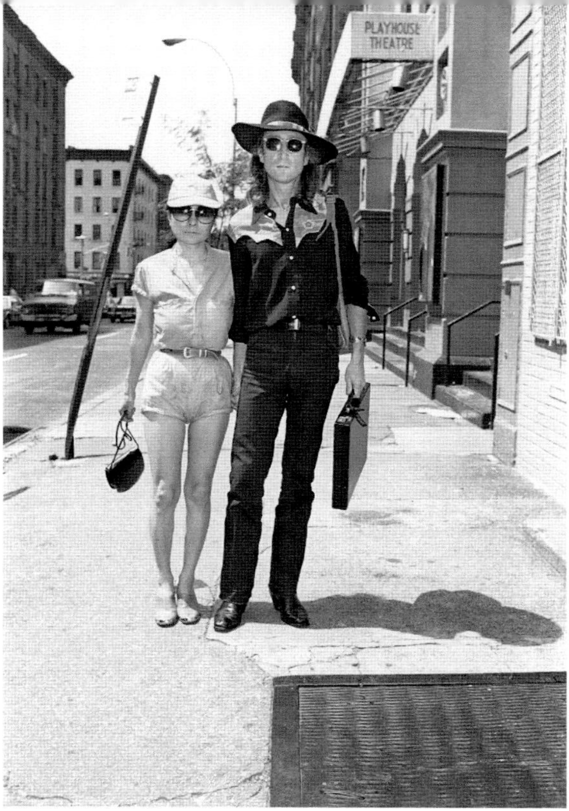

19. John and Yoko photo 7, August 7, 1980.

make out John's face under his wide-brimmed hat. "Looks great," Farrington remarked to the couple. "Let's get one going in." And with that, he clicked the shutter as John paused slightly before stepping onto the front stoop, at the same time capturing Yoko mid-stride, her swinging arm and purse imparting a sense of well-timed movement.

"I was confident I got the shot, casual and candid, with John and Yoko nonchalantly looking over at me," Farrington recalled. If he had captured the image a mere second later, they would have been looking downward, and the shot would have been for naught. That's when Farrington noticed another man's legs just inside the doorway and walking

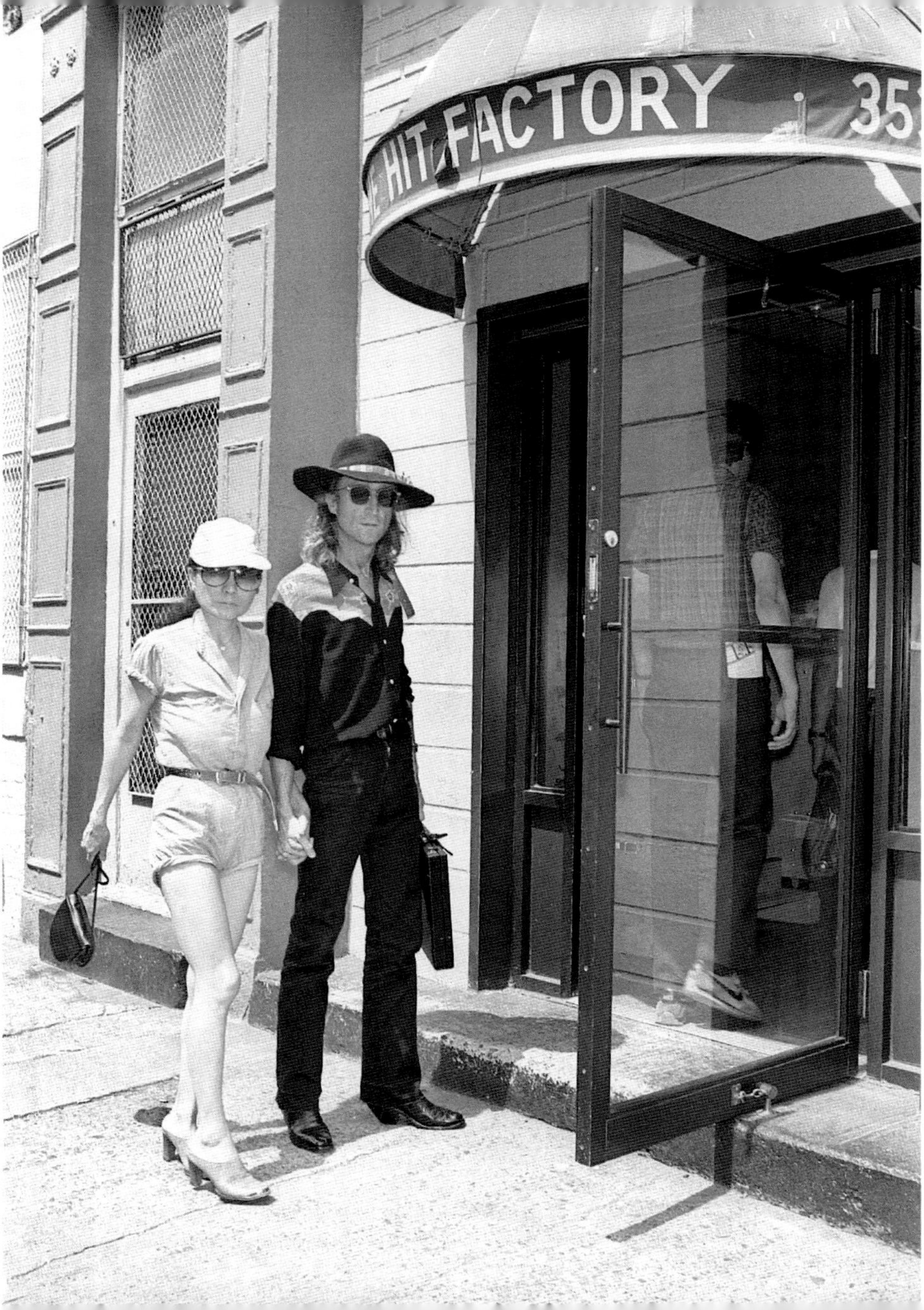

20. John and Yoko photo 8, August 7, 1980.

ahead of the famous clear. "Did the presence of this innocent bystander ruin the image?" Farrington wondered.

But there was no time to think. Following his subjects into the building, Farrington adjusted his eyes to the indoor lighting, which stood in dramatic contrast to the sunny streetscape. "We were moving down a long corridor towards a set of elevator doors," he remembered, "and I could hear soft voices as we passed two partially open doorways. I heard a woman's voice whispering behind me in awestruck amazement, 'Oh my God, that's John Lennon and Yoko Ono!'" Recognizing the futility of trying to keep their mission top-secret, Farrington laughed quietly to himself. "She'd better not tell anybody," he remembered thinking as he scanned the hallway for any evidence of the mysterious bystander who had preceded them into the building.

As John looked on, Farrington adjusted his strobe, shutter speed, and lens aperture settings to account for the comparatively dim indoor lighting and closer proximity to his subjects. As they waited at the end of the hallway, the photographer began to fret about the elevator. Would studio security emerge and demand that he vacate the premises at once? Once again, he reflected on Cohen's cautionary words: "If anyone stops you, you absolutely cannot say, 'I'm with John and Yoko.' You're on your own and have to figure it out." Standing there with the world's most famous musical couple, Farrington began to realize that all of Cohen's cloak-and-dagger instructions were most likely the stuff of nonsense. These were real, flesh-and-blood subjects. A quick glance at Yoko reminded him about how nervous she had been that day. "She may have been in charge," Farrington recalled, "but that also meant that everything rested entirely on her shoulders." In contrast with his wife, John was geared-up and confident, not revealing an iota of nervousness as they waited for the elevator. Farrington observed the couple as they stood close together, shoulder to shoulder, arms touching down to their wrists, with fingers interlocked in an intimate, tight grasp. "Beautiful together hands," he

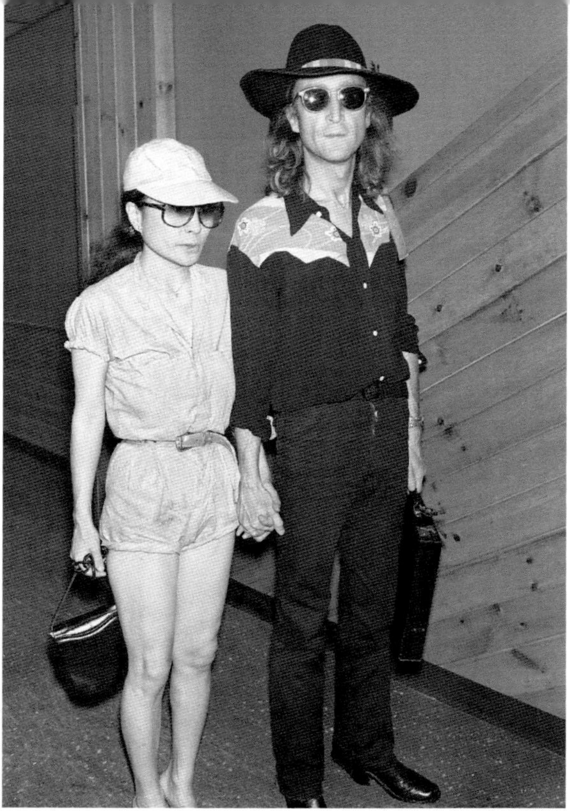

21. John and Yoko photo 9, August 7, 1980.

thought to himself. “I want that photo.” Farrington raised his camera and got the shot just as the elevator doors opened.

When the elevator doors rattled open on the sixth floor, the trio was greeted with the image of a knotty-pine, wood-paneled wall. A large sign announced, “The Hit Factory Recording Studio.” Naturally, it would be the key component in Farrington’s next shot. A photo with the Hit Factory sign might even rival the awning photo outside the studio. With people beginning to make their way over from a nearby lounge, Farrington knew that he had to act quickly. “Excuse me,” he remarked to John and Yoko, “I’d love to get a quick shot in front of the sign please.”

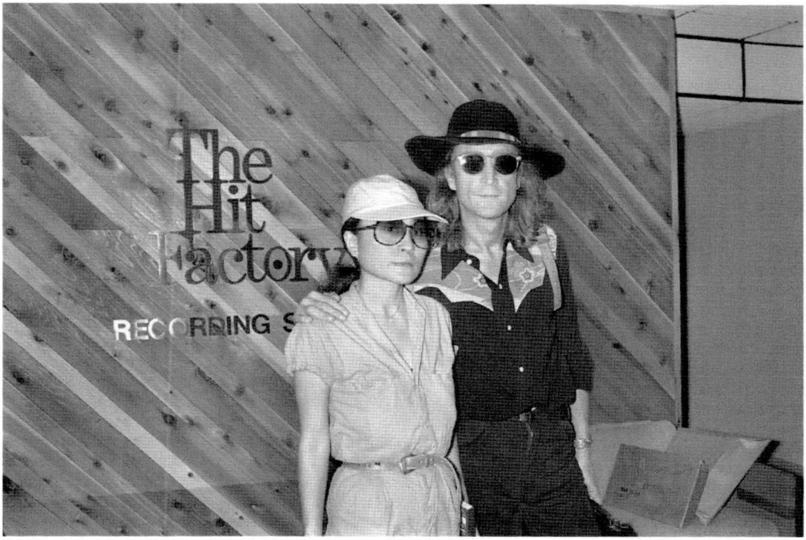

22. John and Yoko photo 10, August 7, 1980.

With that, the couple moved somewhat robotically in front of the sign, and Farrington snapped a horizontal shot.

"Just one more please," he added, holding the camera upright and taking a vertical shot.

As Farrington captured the second image, John quipped in a deep tone of mock-seriousness, "*What?* Are we here to promote the Hit Factory?" By contrast, Yoko sported a dark expression. Would her stoic glare—frowning in her own publicity photos—be amenable to the sort of candid photo that Cohen was hoping to serve as his press release?

After making a few casual greetings, the Lennons went their separate ways. Yoko headed for the studio offices, while John disappeared down a dimly lit corridor. "It felt strange to be left alone, unescorted—apparently to do as I pleased," Farrington later recalled. Shrugging his shoulders, the photographer fell into step behind John as he made his

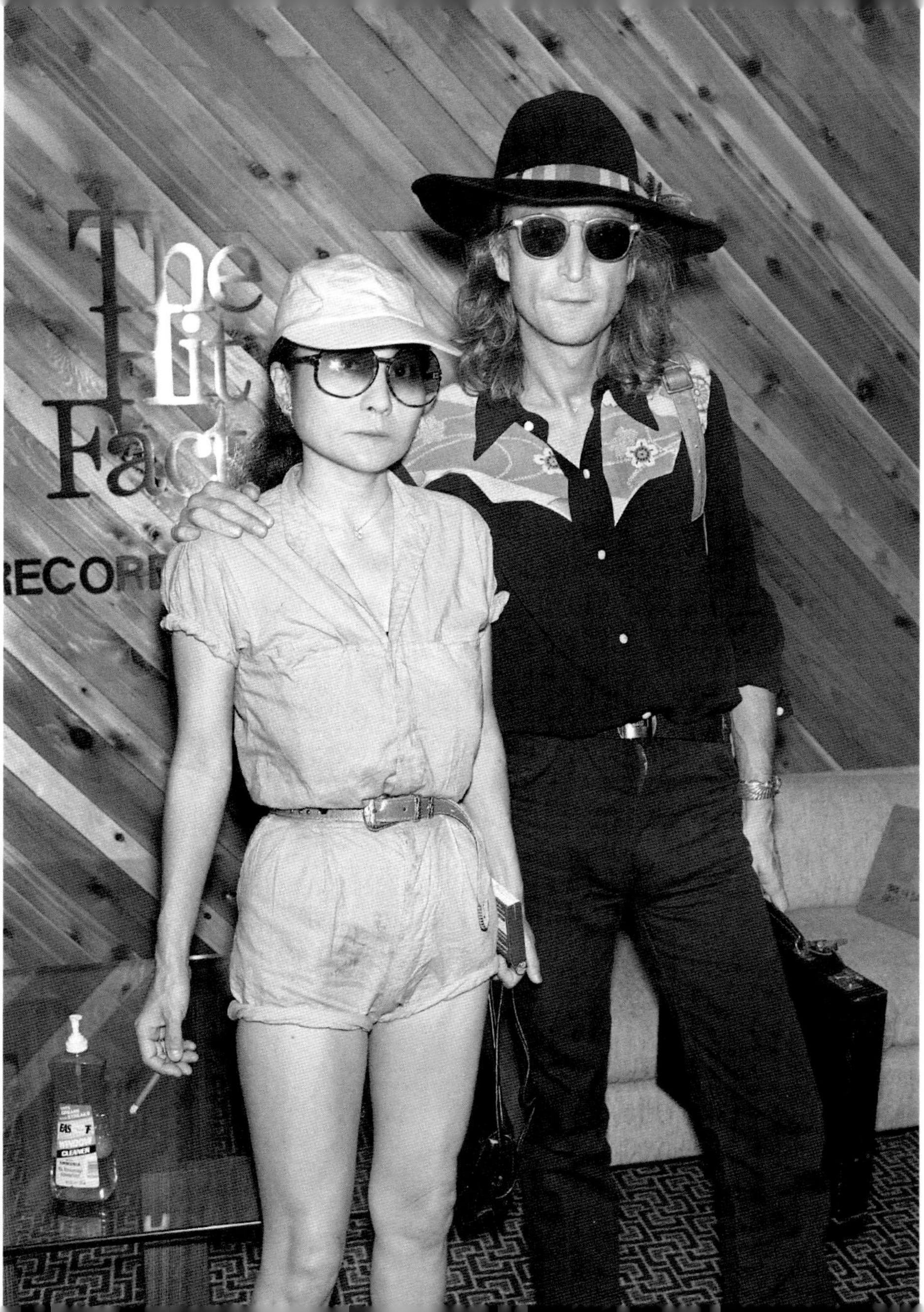

23. John and Yoko photo 11, August 7, 1980.

way into the studio's well-lit control room. Quickly scanning the cramped space for the best shooting angles, he began visualizing a shot of John alone behind the mixing board with a wall of reel-to-reel machines behind him. Struggling to find an optimum shooting angle in front of the mixing desk, Farrington nearly tripped over a small couch. And that's when he caught a glance at the window that divided the booth from the studio floor. "I was surprised by how small and intimate it was," he recalled. "The wood floor was parquet, the walls either knotty-pine paneling or covered with two-foot-wide vertical sections of acoustic material. I could not imagine a warmer, more conducive space for John and Yoko's pent-up musical creativity to emanate."

Adjusting the viewfinder for a short-distance shot, Farrington raised his camera and focused on John, who was in the act of carefully opening up his attaché case, only to discover that he had unclasped it upside down, nearly spilling reams of sheet music onto the floor. After he righted himself, he carefully removed a photograph of Sean from their recent sojourn in Bermuda, which he would later affix inside the control booth above the mixing desk. As John recalled, "I was guilty all through the making of *Double Fantasy*. We had his picture pinned in the studio 'cause I didn't want to lose contact with what I'd got. We had the picture up there all the time in between the speakers so whenever you're checking the stereo, he was looking at me all the time."[2] In the last possible instant, John looked up, and Farrington dutifully captured the shot.

Hearing voices making their way down the corridor to the control room, Farrington took another shot a moment later.

As he took the second photo, Farrington felt Yoko brushing behind him. "Follow me now, through here," she snapped, leading him into a nearby green room. "It was dark and uninteresting," Farrington recalled. "There were maybe two tables, a couple of chairs, a couch, and a mini-fridge. With her back to me as I entered, Yoko was already talking on the telephone, while holding a white Styrofoam coffee cup." He quickly ascertained that she was talking to Cohen and seemingly complaining

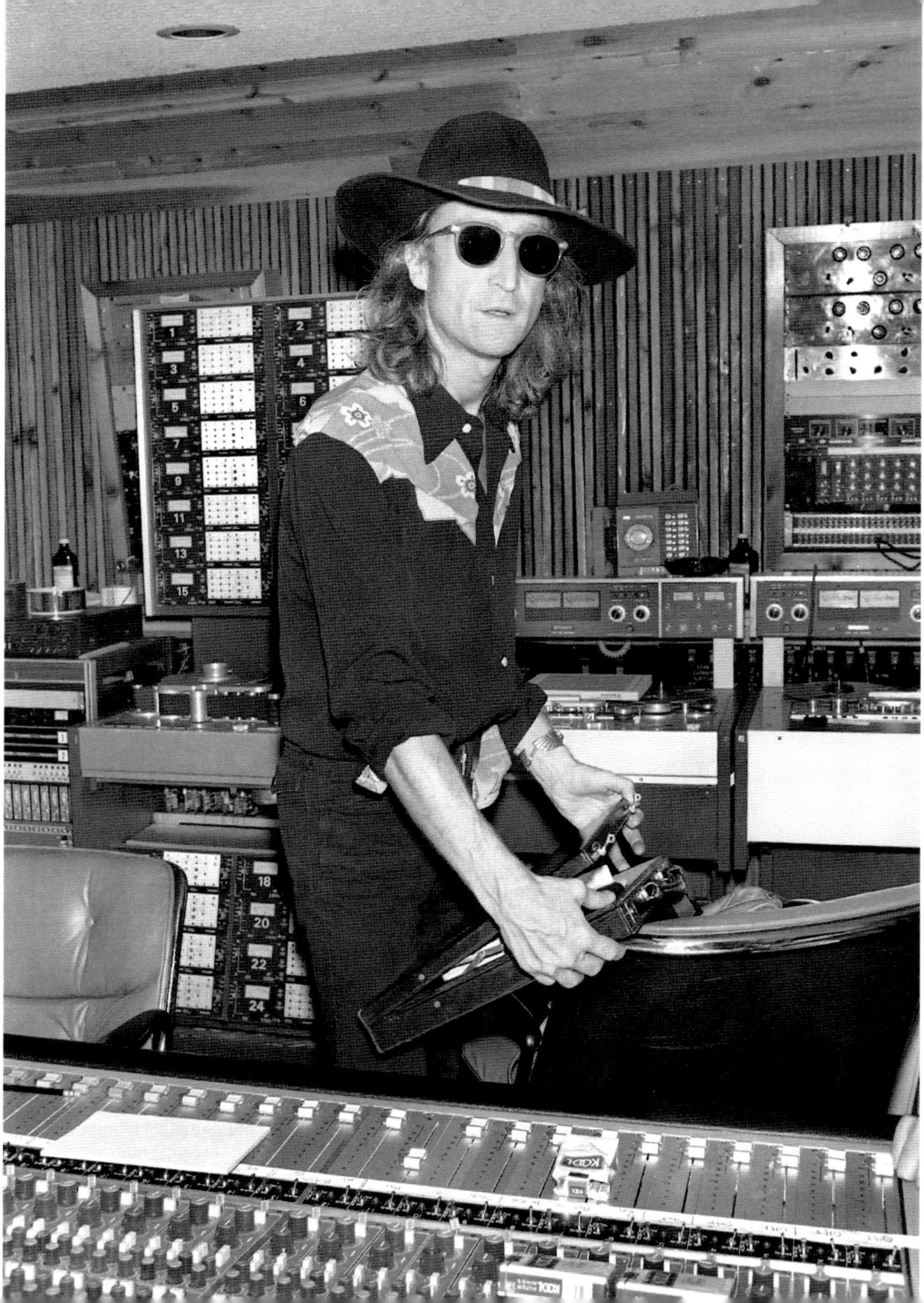

24. John and Yoko photo 12, August 7, 1980.

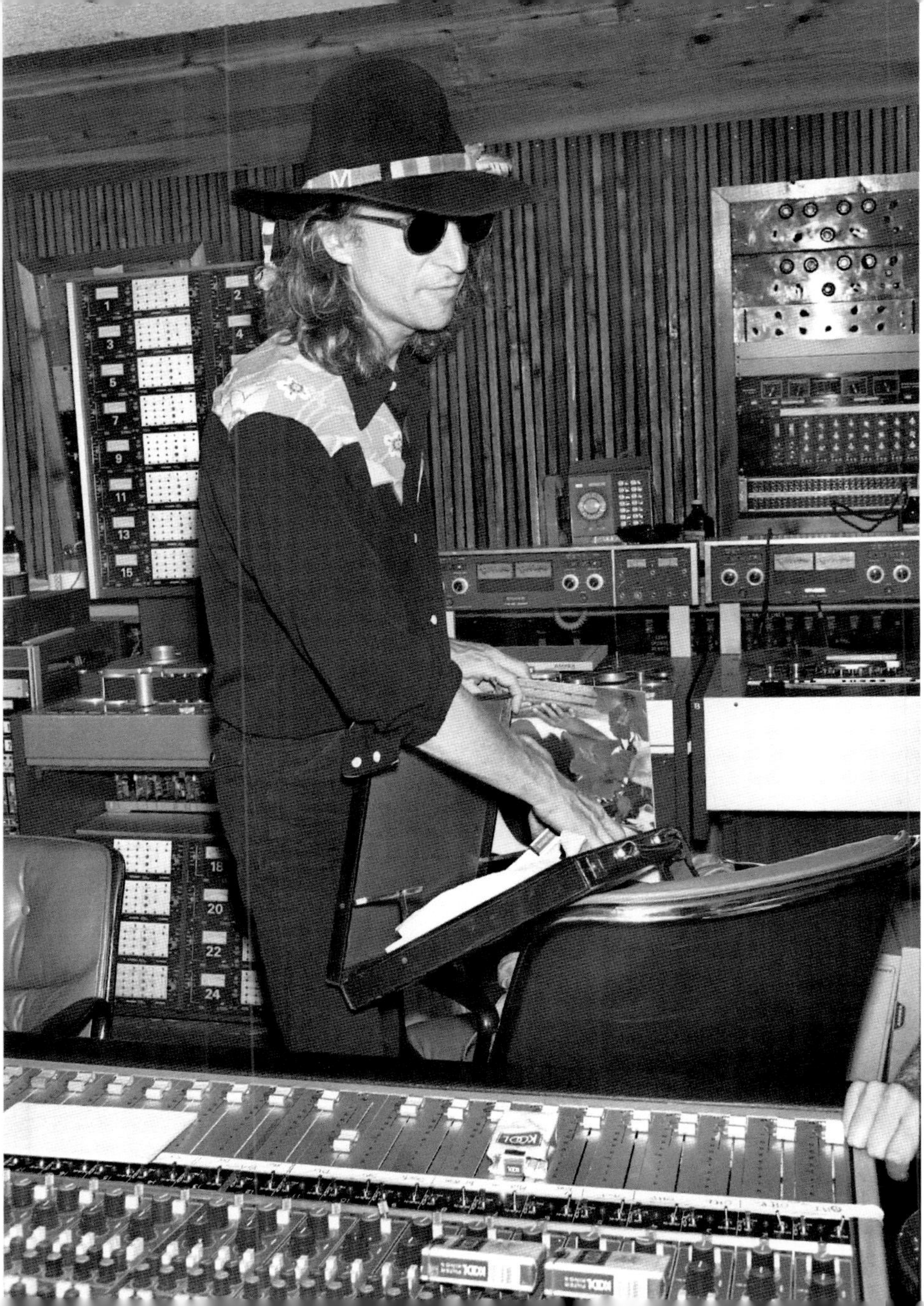

25. John and Yoko photo 13, August 7, 1980.

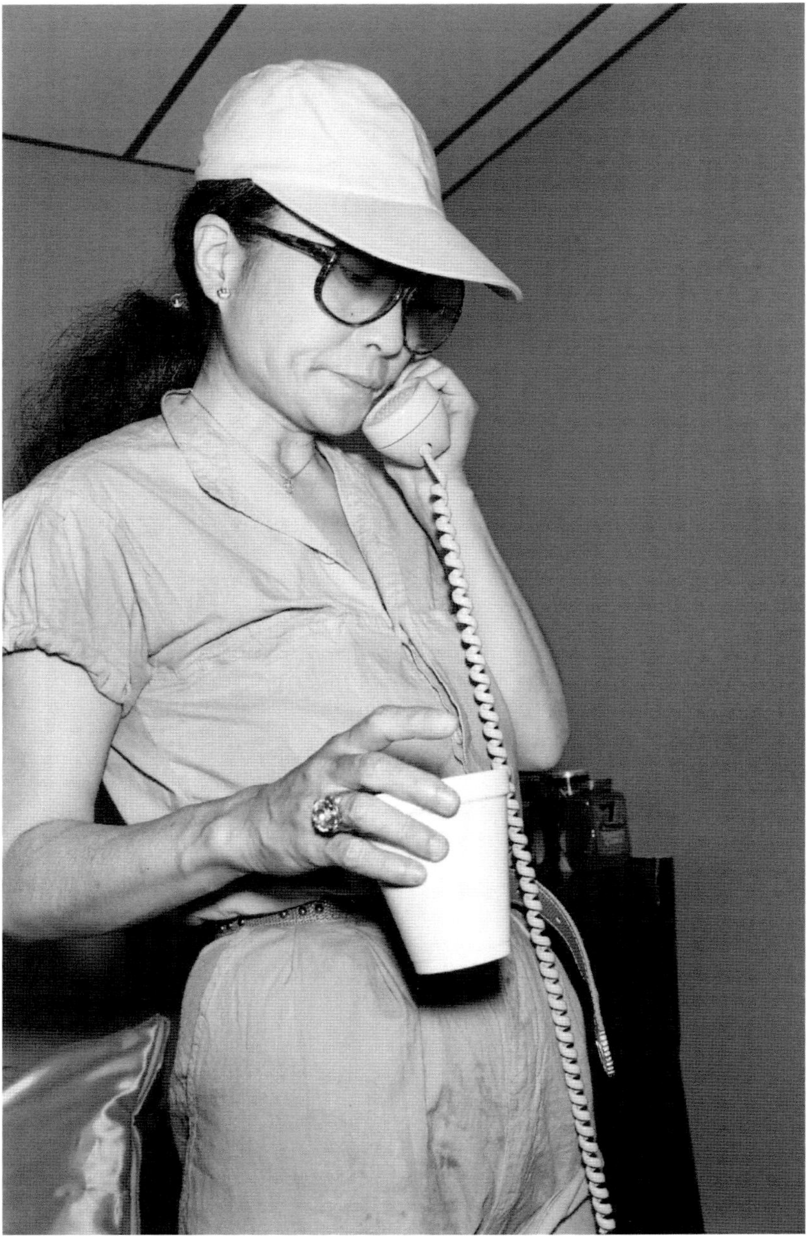

26. John and Yoko photo 14, August 7, 1980.

about him to the PR flak. "Dismissively handing me the receiver with extended arm, Yoko deadpanned, 'He wants to talk to *you*,' as if I was in trouble at school." Feeling relatively confident about the images he had already captured, Farrington told Cohen that "I got at least one decent shot of them leaving the Dakota together hand in hand, and I lined up a nice shot of them entering the Hit Factory outside in the bright sun. It looks candid, and I included the awning above their heads with the Hit Factory clearly showing. I also got posed shots next to the Hit Factory sign right inside the sixth-floor recording studio lobby—those might be cool, too." Pleased with the photographer's progress, Cohen replied, "Sounds good. Do you think you can get something of them in the studio before heading back?"

And that's when Farrington heard it—the roar of an electric guitar emanating from the adjacent studio. He knew that he needed to make his way into the studio as soon as possible. He had never heard anything like the sonic screeches that were suddenly permeating around the sixth floor. But before he could make his escape from the lounge, Yoko stopped him in his tracks. Facing him with the coffee cup resting in her hand while John's loud, piercing guitar notes beckoned nearby, she began lecturing him about the finer points of celebrity photography. "Don't you know that you're supposed to shoot upwards at famous people?" she said. "Don't just photograph John. Take a photo of me. Shoot up at me right now on the phone," she insisted, while holding the receiver in her left hand and balancing the coffee cup in her right.

"Yes, of course," Farrington replied, dropping down onto one knee to accommodate an up-angle composition.

As he looked on, she began punching another number into the telephone. Not knowing what else to do, he politely muttered, "Thanks, Mrs. Lennon. I'll see you in the studio with John. I just need a couple more shots of both of you together before I head back."

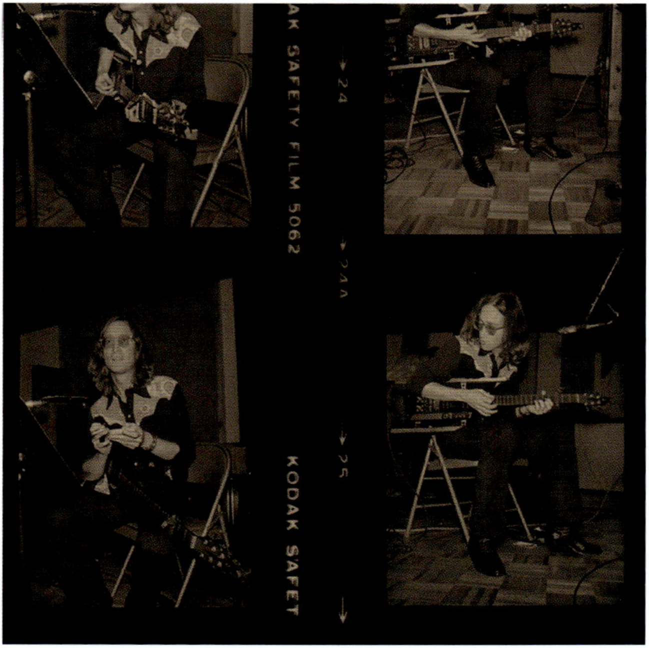
AK SAFETY FILM 5062
KODAK SAFET

7.

The Sardonyx

When Farrington located John on the studio floor a few moments later, he was treated to a most unusual sight. The former Beatle was clutching a futuristic-looking contraption with two stainless-steel outrigger bars dominating its frame. The strange instrument was known as the Sardonyx, which John had taken to calling his "space guitar." Originally built by luthier Jeff Levin and outfitted with custom electronics by Ken Schaffer, the Sardonyx 800 D II guitar was virtually unknown at the time. Having produced some two-dozen Sardonyx guitars over the years, Levin and Schaffer worked out of Matt Umanov's renowned New York City guitar shop. Levin fashioned the body of the guitar out of wood, with the guitar strap attached to the upper aluminum tubing. Schaffer later recalled that John had purchased the instrument himself, having been a regular customer at Umanov's Lower Manhattan store.[1]

That December, as John and Yoko conducted their media blitz associated with the *Double Fantasy* album, Lennon waxed nostalgic about the eccentric instrument.

> "I bought this beautiful electric guitar 'round about the period I got back with Yoko and had the baby," he explained to *Rolling*

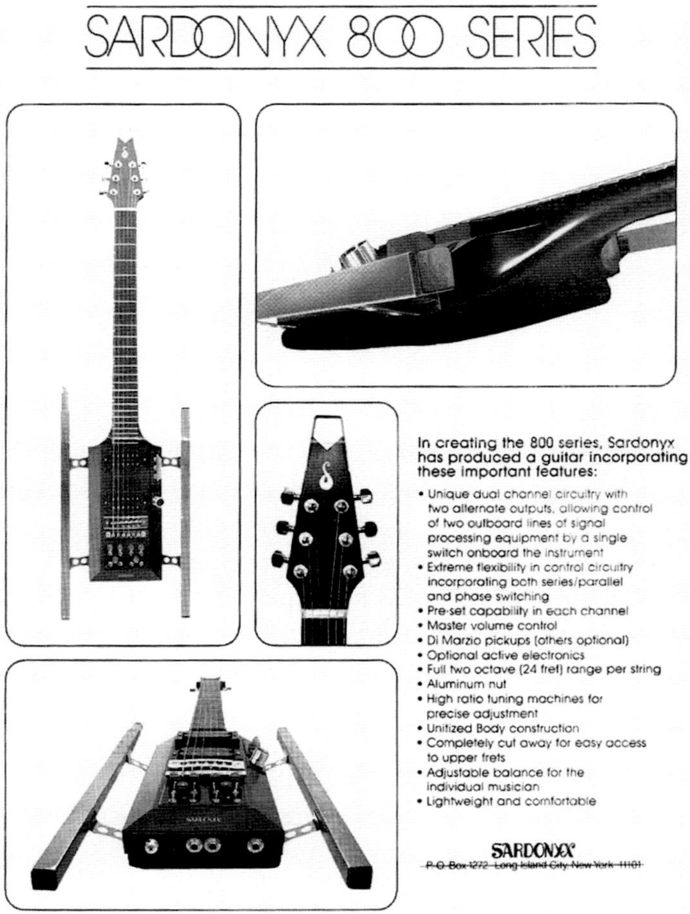

27. Sardonyx advertisement, ca. 1978.

> *Stone*'s Jonathan Cott. "It's not a normal guitar; it doesn't have a body; it's just an arm and this tubelike, toboggan-looking thing, and you can lengthen the top for the balance of it if you're sitting or standing up." After purchasing it during the mid-1970s, "I played it a little, then just hung it up behind the bed, but I'd look at it every now and then because it had never done a professional thing, it had never really been played. I didn't want to hide it the way one would hide an instrument because it was too painful to look at—like Artie Shaw went through a big thing and never played again. But I used to look at it and think, 'Will I ever pull it down?' Next to it on the wall I'd placed the number 9 and a dagger Yoko had given me—a dagger made out of a bread knife from the American Civil War to cut away the bad vibes, to cut away the past symbolically. It was just like a picture that hangs there but you never really see, and then recently I realized, 'Oh, goody! I can finally find out what this guitar is all about,' and I took it down and used it in making *Double Fantasy*."[2]

Standing nearby in the studio, Farrington observed in awe as John continued strumming the Sardonyx, which emitted an explosive, howling fusillade of electronic sound. "The unusual sounds that this unique-looking instrument was producing under Lennon's famous fingers was unlike anything I had ever heard musically," Farrington recalled, "certainly nothing remotely Beatles-esque—even in their most experimental phases. The otherworldly sounds were only matched by the guitar's alien look and design." Having removed his wide-brimmed hat and traded in his shades for a pair of eyeglasses, John was standing tall in the recording studio, guitar slung low over his shoulder, amplifier at his feet, warming up alone in the heart of the Hit Factory, save for Farrington and Fred, who was gingerly setting up Lennon's acoustic guitars nearby.

Realizing that John was posing for his benefit, Farrington was determined to capture images of him playing the bizarre instrument—with or without Yoko in tow. While John continued wailing away on the Sardonyx, pausing occasionally to activate a series of foot pedals with his boots, Farrington took a vertical shot of the musician as Yoko entered the frame and opened the attaché case. As she rifled through some papers, John looked up with a quizzical expression, as if he had recognized someone. "It was my first shot of John and Yoko working in the studio," Farrington realized, "but it wasn't a great one. It was way too candid."

And that's when John abruptly stopped playing, raising his arms to greet another musician across the studio floor. It made for an incredible image, and Farrington dutifully clicked the shutter.

The photographer didn't know it at the time, but he had captured John in the act of greeting studio musician Earl Slick. For his part, Slick had big plans that day, hoping to be the first to arrive at the Hit Factory in a display of earnestness and responsibility. But he had been shown up by John, of all people—the very person whom he had most hoped to impress that day. "I couldn't believe it!" said Slick, having seen his plans thwarted so quickly. As he walked up to introduce himself to John, he was stunned by Lennon's warm-hearted, ebullient greeting. "Nice to see you again!" John exclaimed. "I was like, 'nice to see you, too, but we haven't met,'" Slick recalled. John assured the young guitarist that his memory must be faulty, that they had in point of fact met during the sessions for David Bowie's *Young Americans* LP.[3]

"Trust me," Slick laughed. "You're a Beatle. If we'd worked together before, I would have remembered it." As for the Bowie sessions, "we must have recorded at different times," Slick added. "No," said John, "we were there together." For Slick, there was only one possibility. "Maybe I was fucking stoned," he replied. "Well," said John, "that's a possibility." If Slick thought that the matter had suddenly concluded in John's mind, he would shortly learn that he was sorely mistaken. As a running joke throughout the *Double Fantasy* sessions, John frequently asked "remember me now?" to Earl as an ongoing jibe.[4]

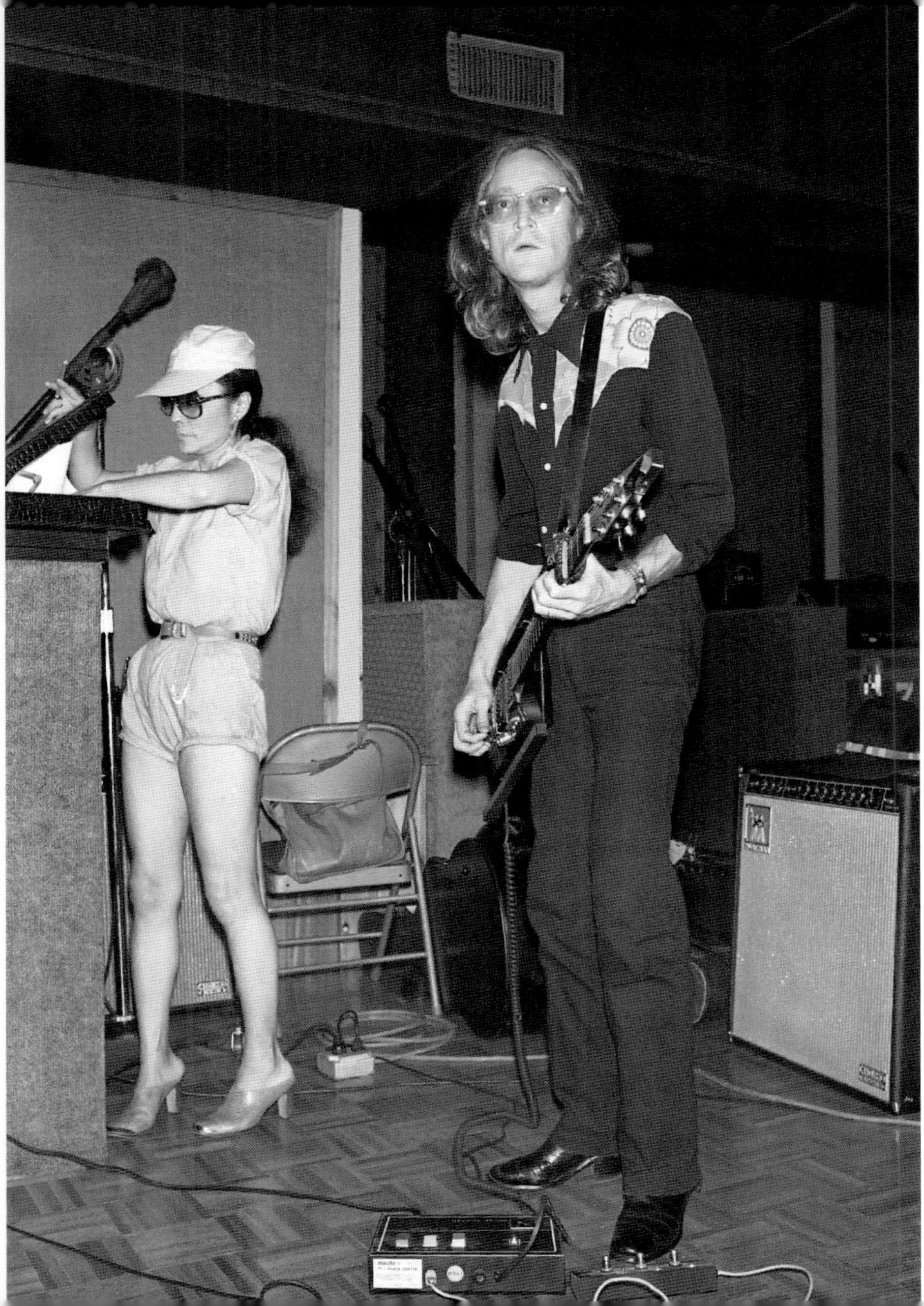

28. John and Yoko photo 15, August 7, 1980.

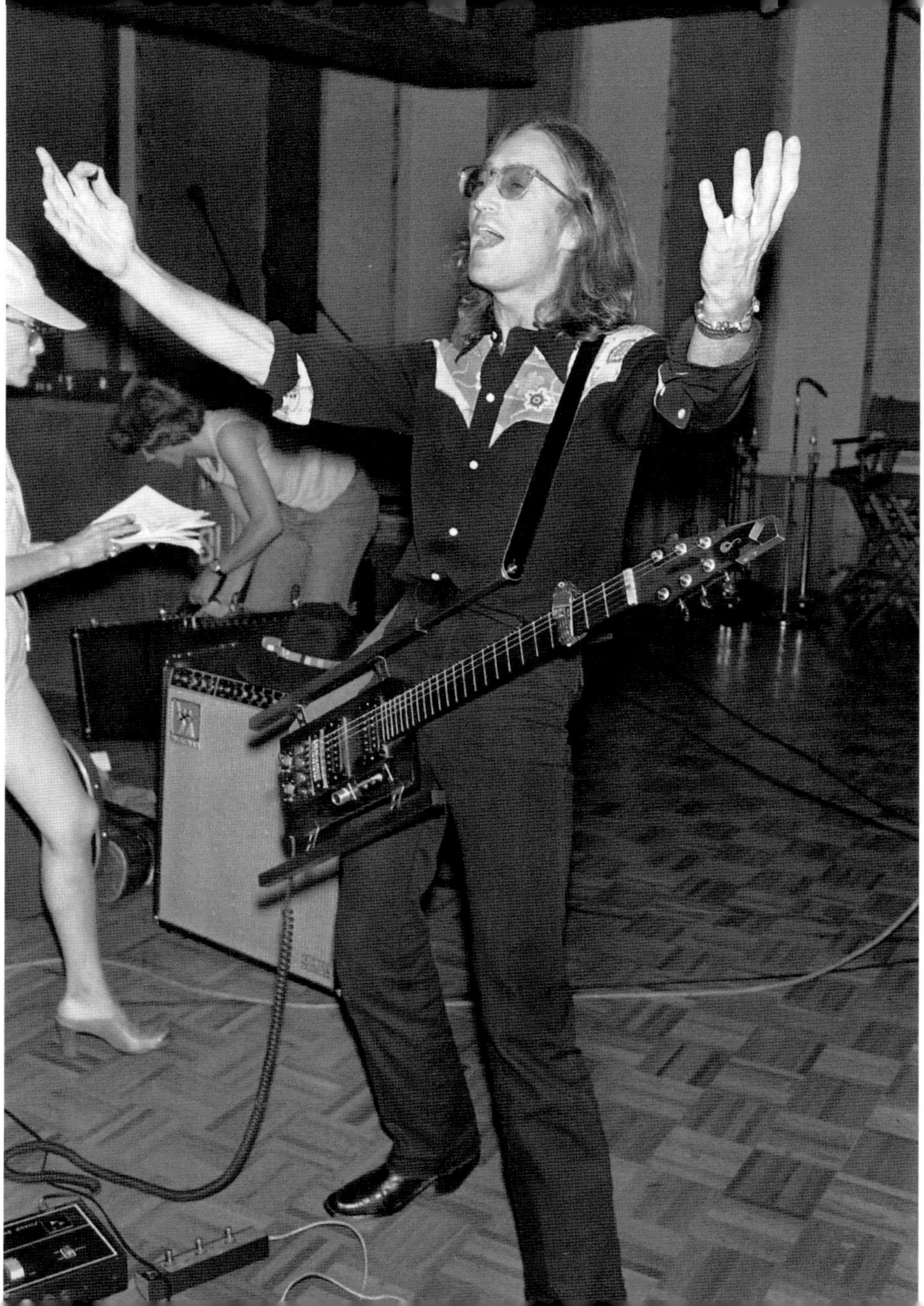

29. John and Yoko photo 16, August 7, 1980.

Not surprisingly, the Sardonyx was already the talk of the Hit Factory. When he first laid eyes on it, Slick said that it looked "like a fucking ski rack for a car!" For his part, Douglas playfully called it the "Sardonicus."[5] By this juncture, Farrington realized that he had already accrued some ninety minutes with John and Yoko—far more than he had originally hoped. The photographer was still mystified after his conversation with Yoko back in the green room, but he was as determined as ever to get a two-shot of the couple. At this point, Yoko was seated comfortably behind John on a high-backed padded stool. "She appeared aloof yet more relaxed with one of her dark brown Nat Sherman cigarettes dangling between her lips," Farrington observed. "She looked cool and camera ready." With two-shots in the offing, Farrington captured a pair of images in quick succession. Up first was a shot of John in a pensive mood, his guitar in hand.

Framing Yoko vertically on the stool, Farrington captured the second shot as she raised her lighter to ignite another Nat Sherman.

He was especially pleased that he had managed to photograph her with an upward trajectory in keeping with her preferences. Moments later, as the studio began filling with musicians slated for the 2:00 P.M. recording session, he shot another exposure of Yoko calmly exhaling cigarette smoke while gazing off into the distance.

Knowing that he only a had a few more minutes to capture the artists at work, Farrington made conversation with Yoko, hoping to set up some additional two-shots before heading back to Boston. "So how's the record going to work?" Farrington asked her. "We're not sure yet," she curtly answered. "One side might be his, the other mine. Or we might alternate songs." Farrington smiled, shifting gears. "That sounds really cool," he replied. "Would you mind if I moved your chair closer to John? I'd like to try a couple more shots before I leave." Meanwhile, out of the corner of his eye, Farrington caught sight of John warming up his vocal cords while still strumming the Sardonyx. John's stance appeared awkward, the photographer thought, but he looked like he was singing. He quickly snapped another image.

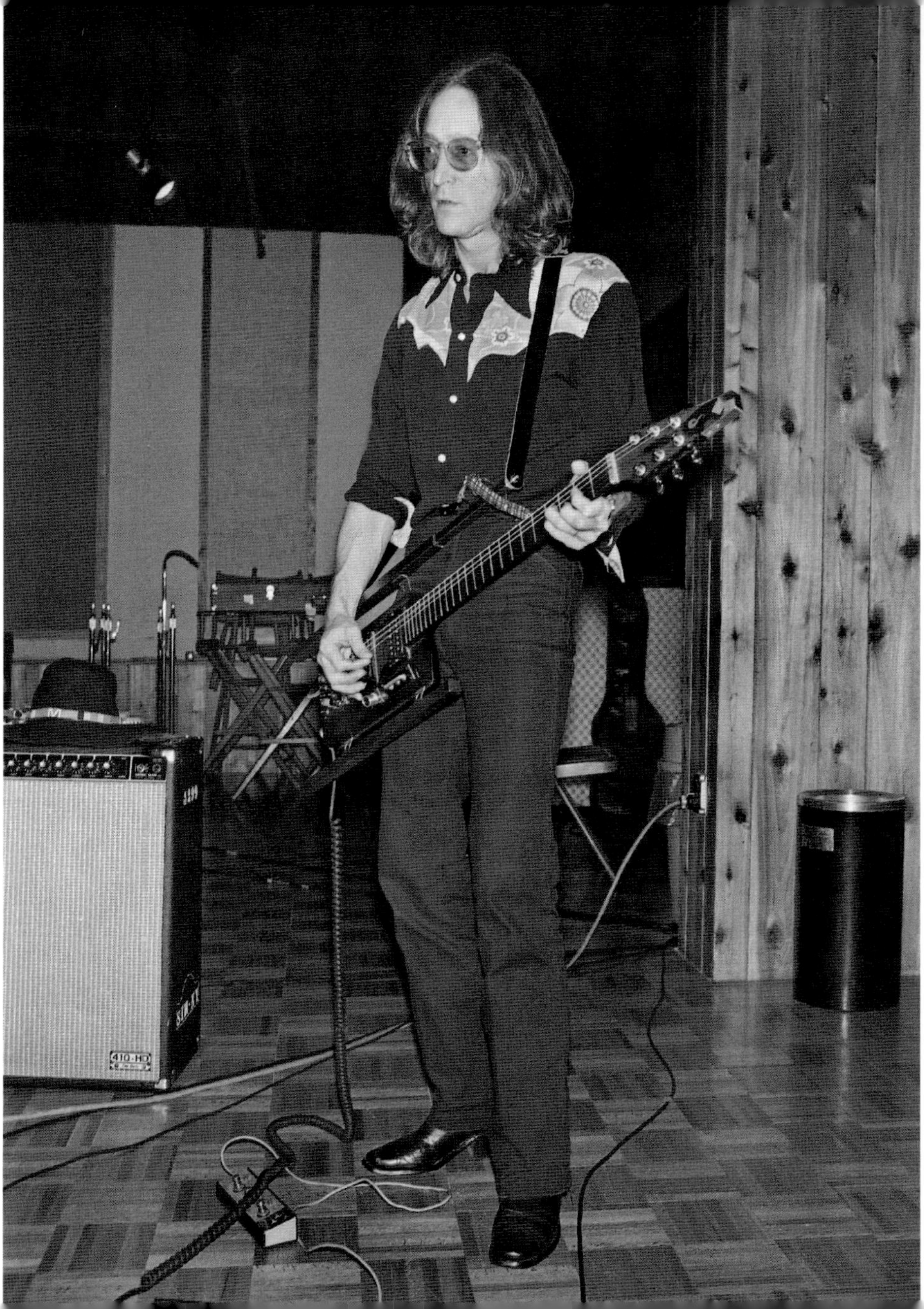

30. John and Yoko photo 17, August 7, 1980.

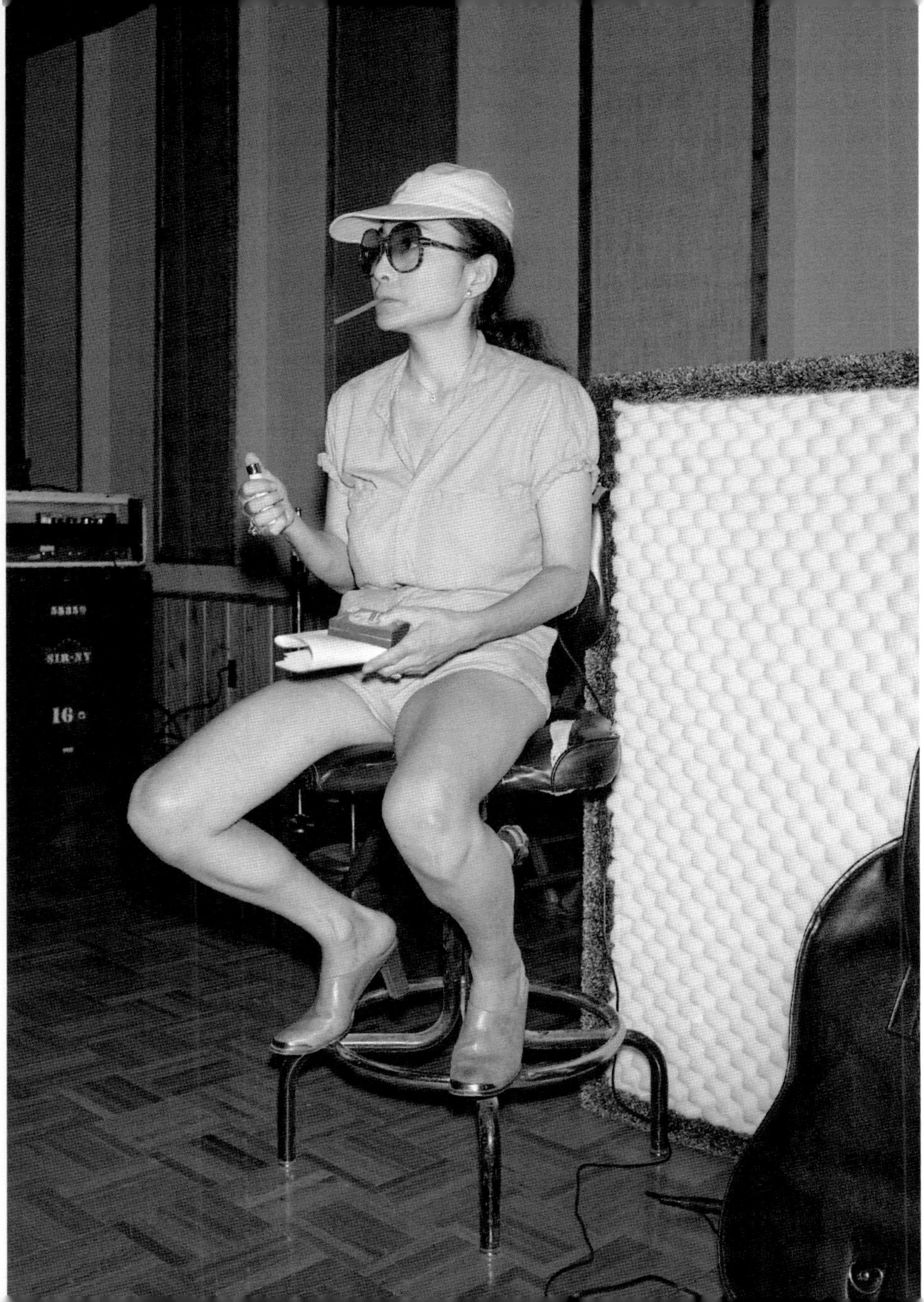

31. John and Yoko photo 18, August 7, 1980.

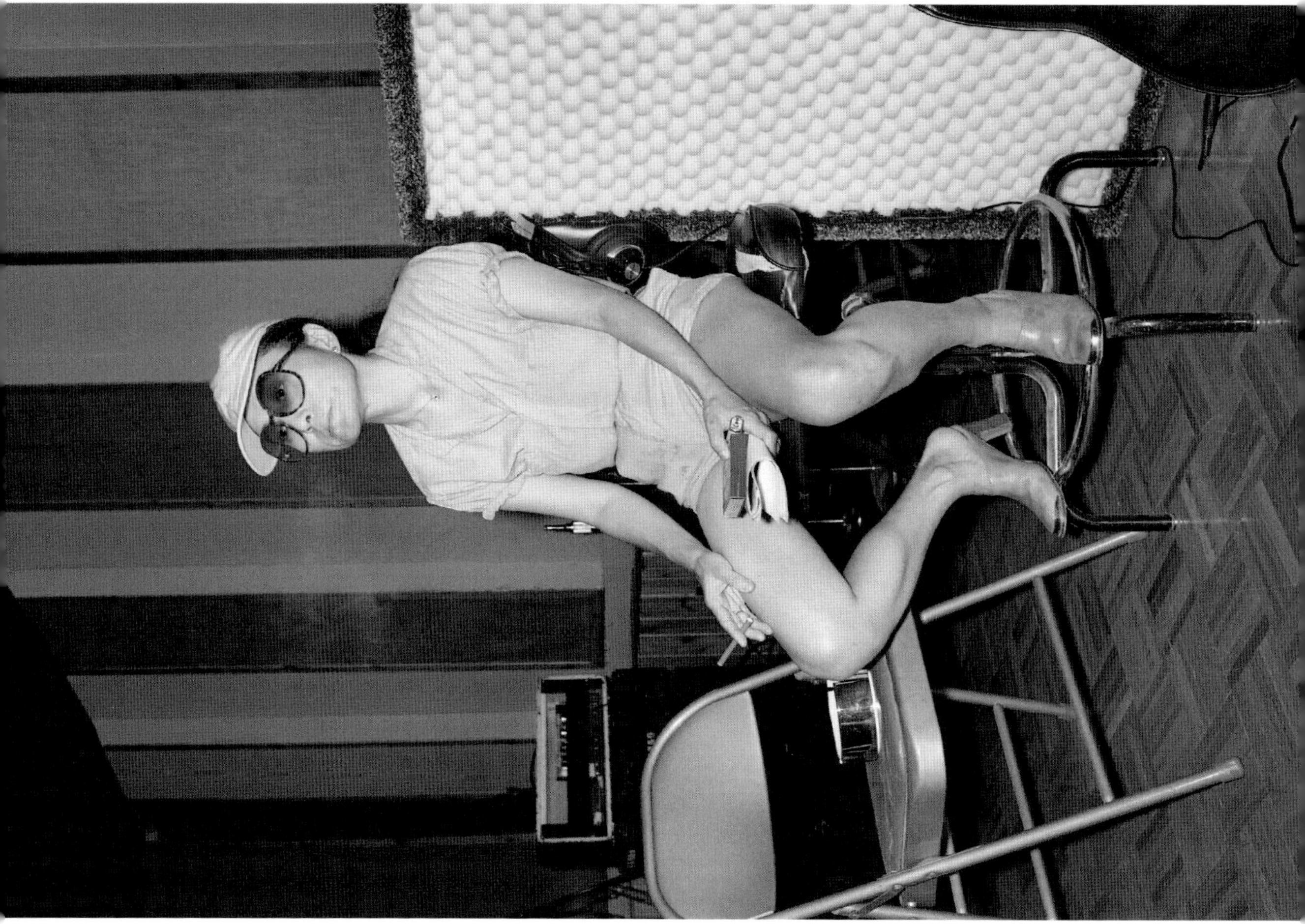

32. John and Yoko photo 19, August 7, 1980.

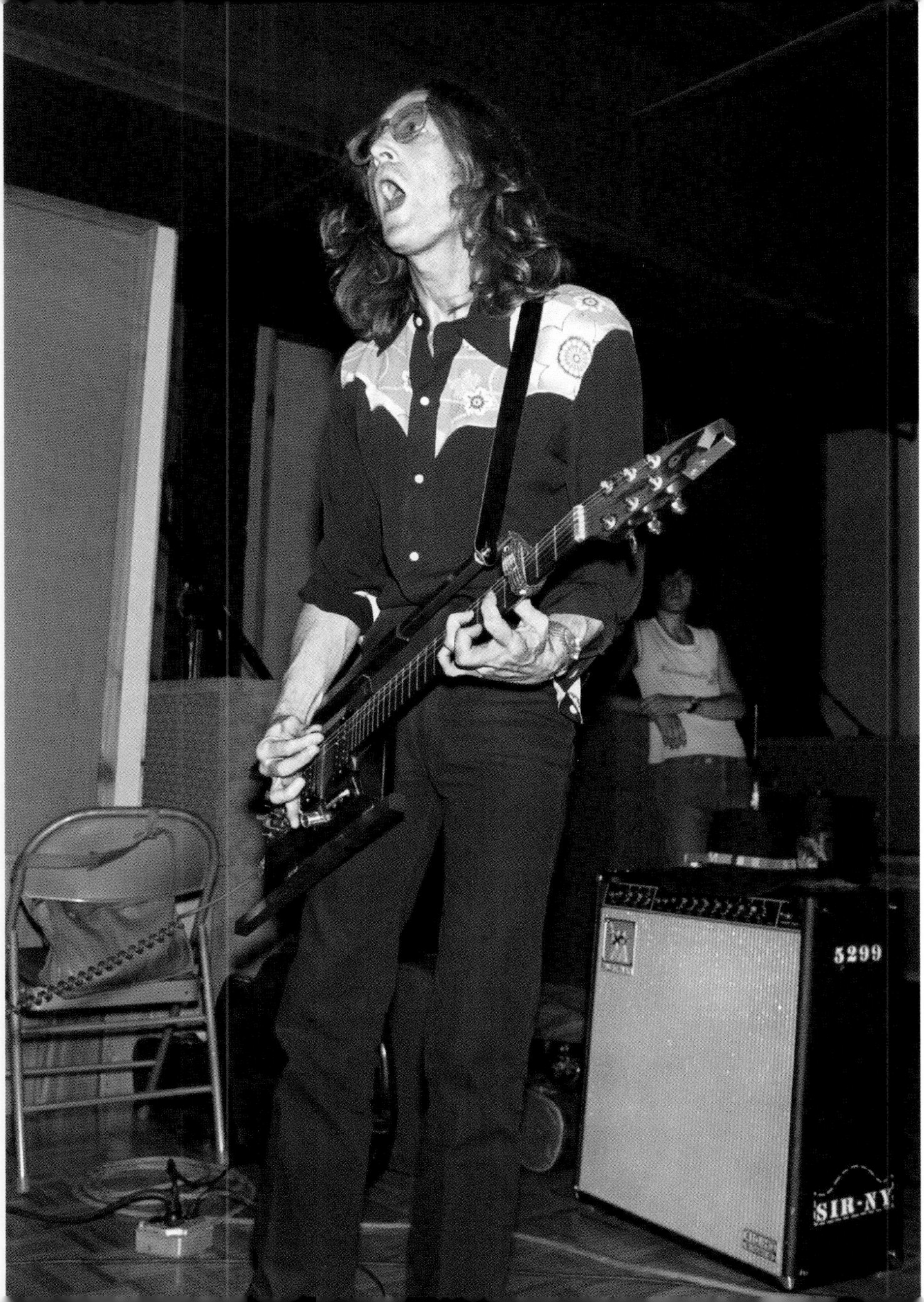

33. John and Yoko photo 20, August 7, 1980.

That's when Farrington happened upon an idea. "Okay," he thought, dismissing his last shot, "time to move some chairs." Carefully stepping over some wires, he moved an old, canvas director's chair a few feet, positioning it just behind the amp on John's left. As if on cue, Yoko, her cigarette still smoldering between her fingers, climbed off her stool and settled into the director's chair. While John continued noodling away on his guitar, Farrington dropped to one knee. Yoko seemed relaxed, slouching slightly in her director's chair, although several inches higher than John, who was seated in front of her. "Oh my Lord," Farrington suddenly realized. "I'm shooting directly between Yoko's bare legs." Salvation arrived when he recognized that carefully positioning his wide-angle lens would allow him to conceal the space between Yoko's knees with the Sardonyx. He clicked the shutter yet again. Crisis averted.

While his gambit with the director's chair had worked its magic, Farrington knew that he still needed to improve the composition. Spotting a tall black ashtray in a corner of the studio, he concocted a new plan. He decided to move the object into the shot. Standing up and retrieving the ashtray, he crossed strategically behind Yoko's chair and firmly grasped the two wooden supports behind her shoulders. "I just need to move your chair a bit," he explained, and with a soft lurch he was able to pivot Yoko's chair a few inches toward John's amp. It wasn't much of an adjustment, but with the ashtray in the frame, he felt as if he had improved her appearance considerably. Either way, "it was now or never," he thought. "I lowered myself into an uncomfortable crouch and captured their faces together in a two-shot."

Still concentrating on the Sardonyx, John evinced a confident expression, revealing his open-collar neck and a heart-shaped gold necklace. Fab Four geek that he was, Farrington couldn't help noticing the scar on John's neck, the result of a July 1969 automobile accident that he and Yoko, along with their young children Julian and Kyoko, had suffered during a break from the production of the Beatles' *Abbey Road* LP. As Farrington observed the couple in the Hit Factory, Yoko rested her elbows

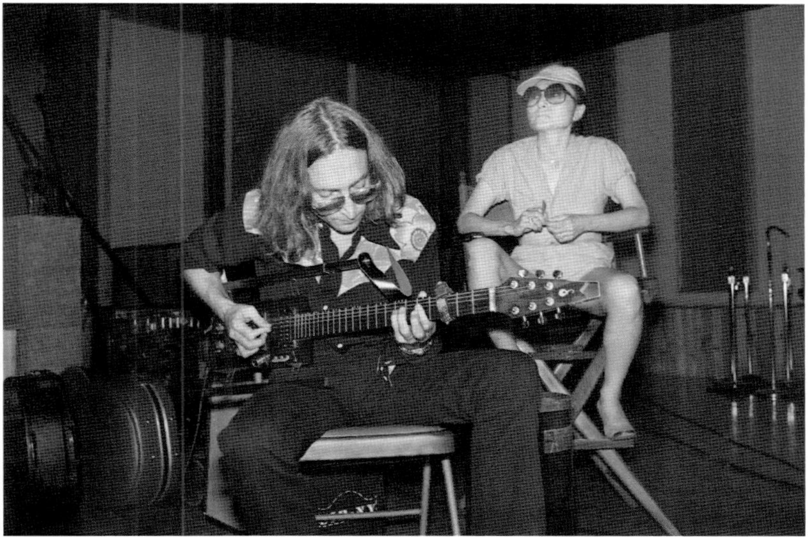

34. John and Yoko photo 21, August 7, 1980.

on the armrest and gazed in her husband's direction. "It was the best double-pose I was likely to get," he figured. As he took the shot, he noticed tiny swirls of smoke rising off Yoko's cigarette.

Moments later, while John continued strumming away on the space-age guitar, his lips pursed with concentration, Farrington clicked the shutter yet again.

With the session shortly set to begin, Yoko took her leave as the Hit Factory's engineers started setting up microphones. Taking his cue, Farrington returned the director's chair back to its original spot and slid the ashtray into a far corner of the studio. But there was John, wailing away on the Sardonyx. With a boom mic now positioned in front of him, he looked every bit the portrait of a rock star in his prime. "With those cool black boots anchoring the shot," Farrington opted to capture another vertical image. In truth, "there was no way I could resist a couple more

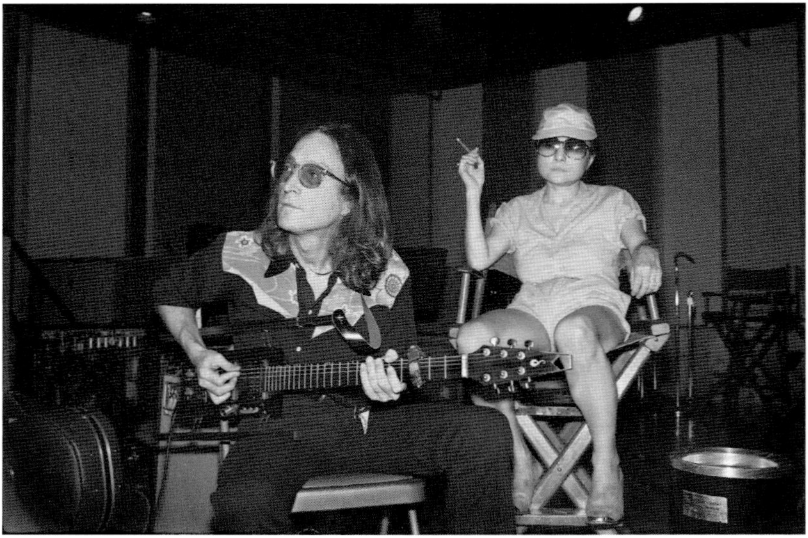

35. John and Yoko photo 22, August 7, 1980.

exposures." As John sang into the microphone, the photographer could feel the back of his neck tingling. To Farrington's mind, "this was, by far, the most amazing shot of the day." Arranger Tony Davilio can be seen in the background, handing out lead sheets.

A half second later, Farrington took yet another shot as John, mouth closed, seemed to lose himself in the music.

Finally, in one of the few instances that afternoon, Farrington felt that he had truly achieved that much-vaunted conspiracy between subject and photographer. "John's posing, but not looking at the camera," he thought to himself. "It's perfect." Checking his film counter, he was surprised that he had only captured twenty-five images. "Would that be enough?" he wondered. Farrington could already hear Cohen's voice ringing in his ears: "Is that all? *One roll?*" But the photographer knew in his heart that it was vital not to overshoot when it came to publicity

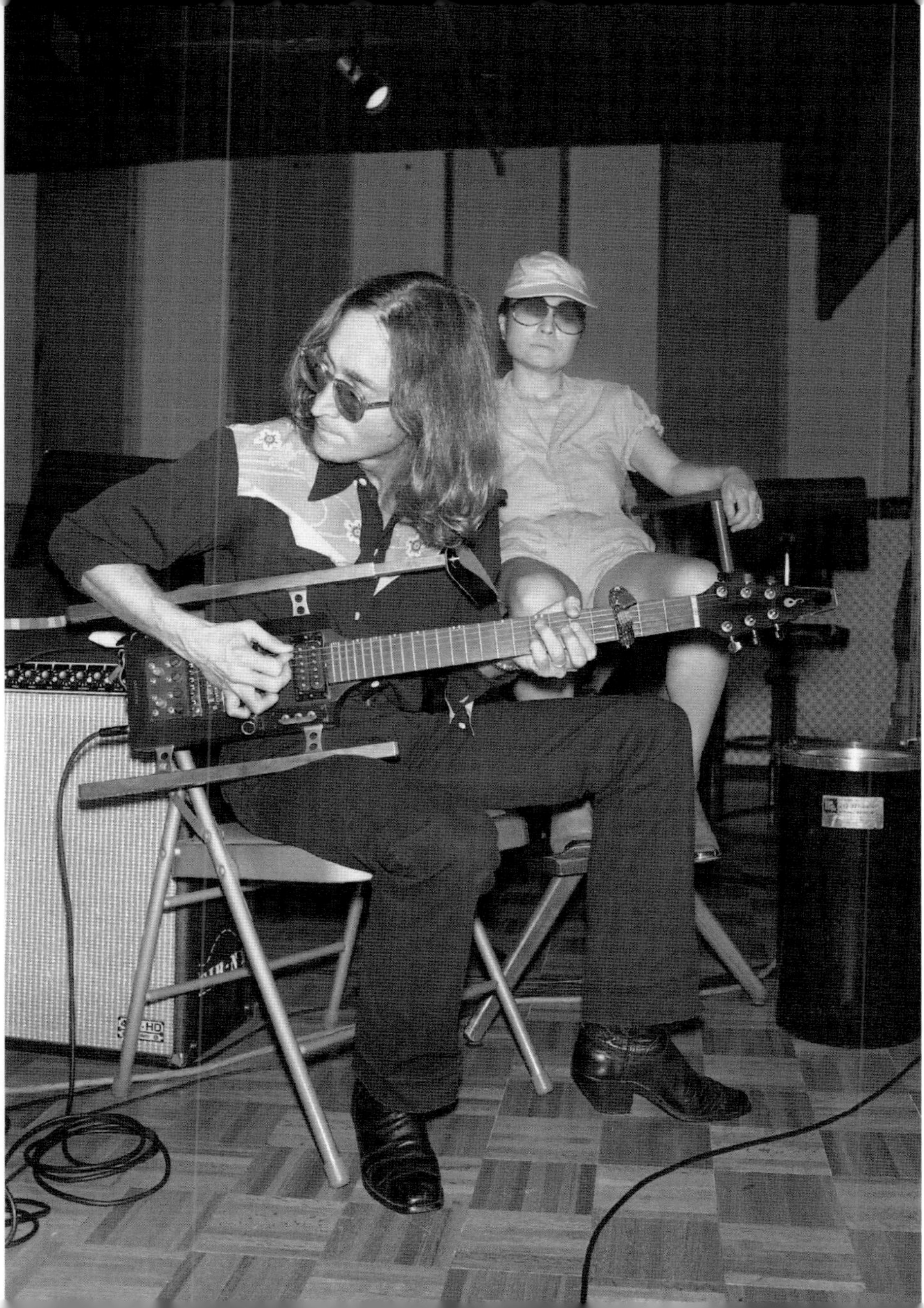

36. John and Yoko photo 23, August 7, 1980.

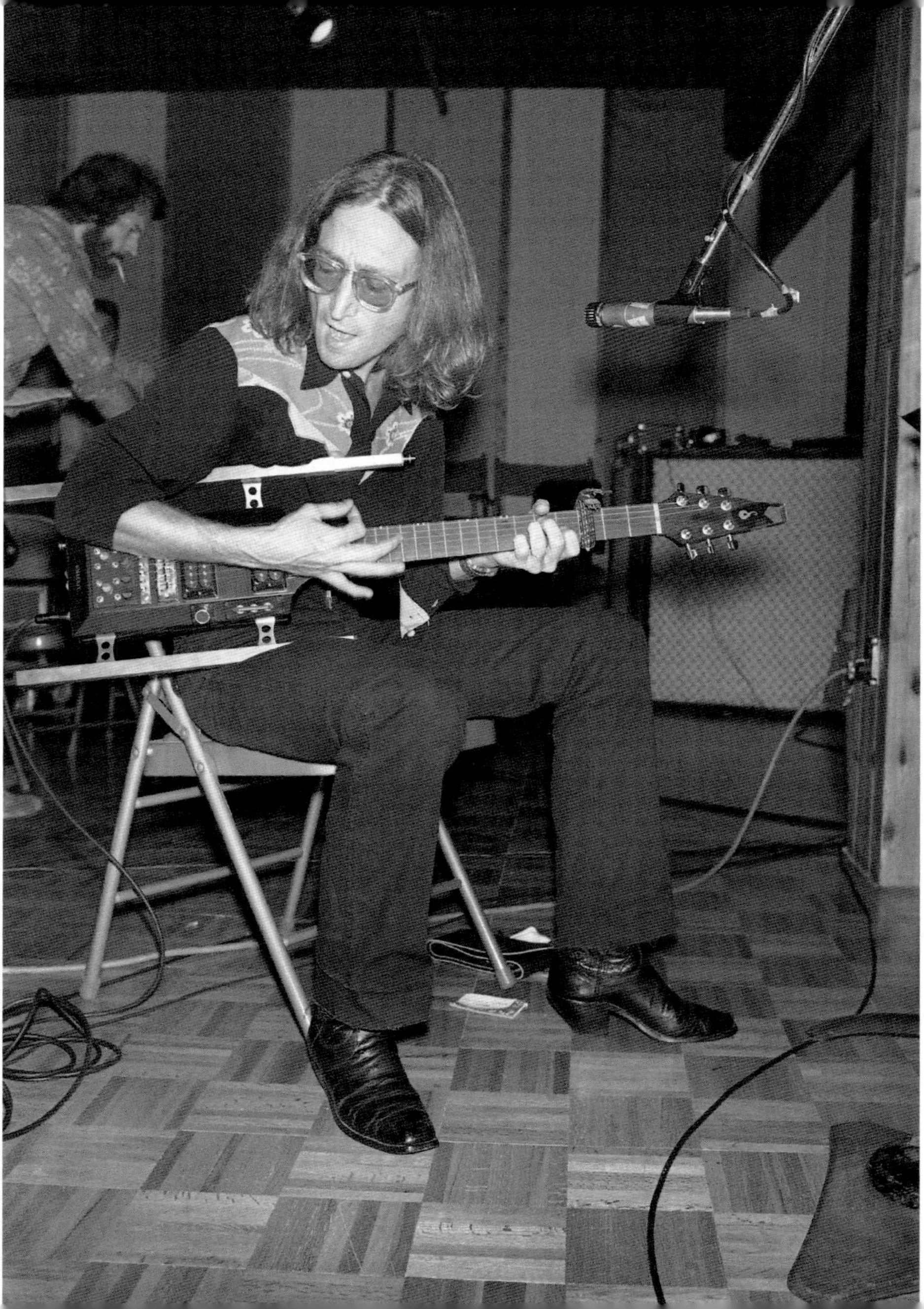

37. John and Yoko photo 24, August 7, 1980.

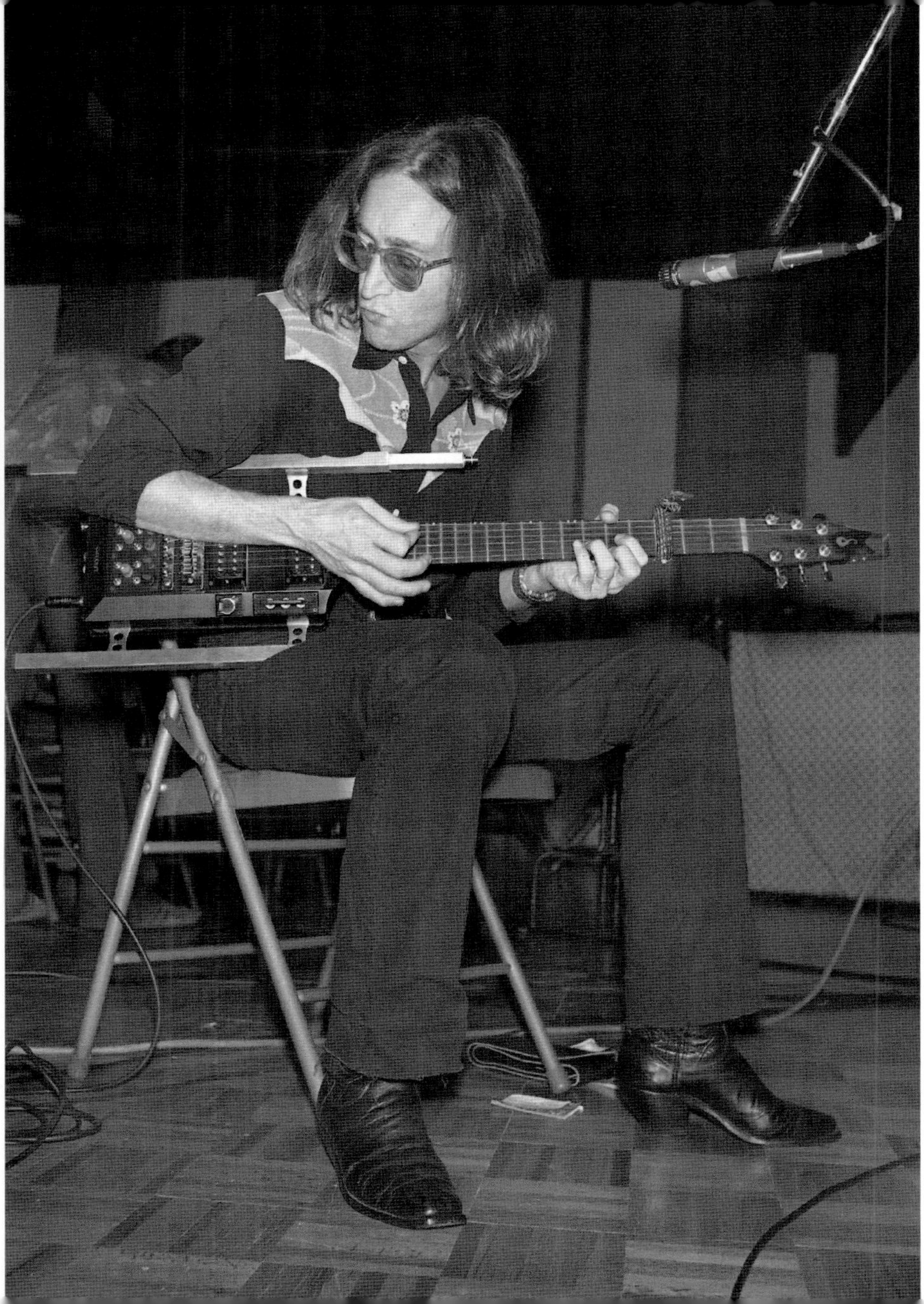

38. John and Yoko photo 25, August 7, 1980.

work. After all, his photo session with Senator Jacob Javits required only a couple of frames. And that shoot had landed Farrington in the pages of *Time* magazine!

By the time Yoko came back into the room, studio personnel had begun setting up music stands for the Lennons' bandmates. Farrington took another opportunity to capture the image of John in quiet repose.[6]

And that's when Yoko stepped back into the frame, positioning herself between her husband and the music stand. She was visibly less tense than earlier. Hoping to take full advantage of her relaxed demeanor, Farrington clicked the shooter as John motioned to his wife with his left hand.

As Douglas and the musicians joined him in the studio, John smiled and quipped that "the photographer was me wife's idea." Farrington realized that the clock was ticking, that he had to make his way back to LaGuardia. Yet he also knew that John was in a jocular mood, that there was still another great shot to be had that day. For a moment, the photographer believed that he had missed his moment—the opportunity to catch the ex-Beatle in an instance of pure joy. But then, "John's laughing eyes met mine as I pivoted in his direction," Farrington recalled. "With my strobe power switched to low, I swooped down on John, lunging to within four feet of his face. Slightly turning away as I made the shot, he smiled broadly."

The candid image of John's grinning face was surely one of the day's highlights.

Farrington was understandably chuffed at having captured John's engaging smile in a moment of unchecked exuberance. As John prepared to take a cigarette break, Farrington hit upon another idea. "You look great," said Farrington, as his subject prepared to light up one of his pungent French Gitanes. "Let me get a quick portrait of you, and maybe one more with Yoko before I head out to meet my deadline." As quickly as John replied, "Okay, man," Farrington positioned his camera and captured the image of John glancing over his shoulder in Yoko's direction.

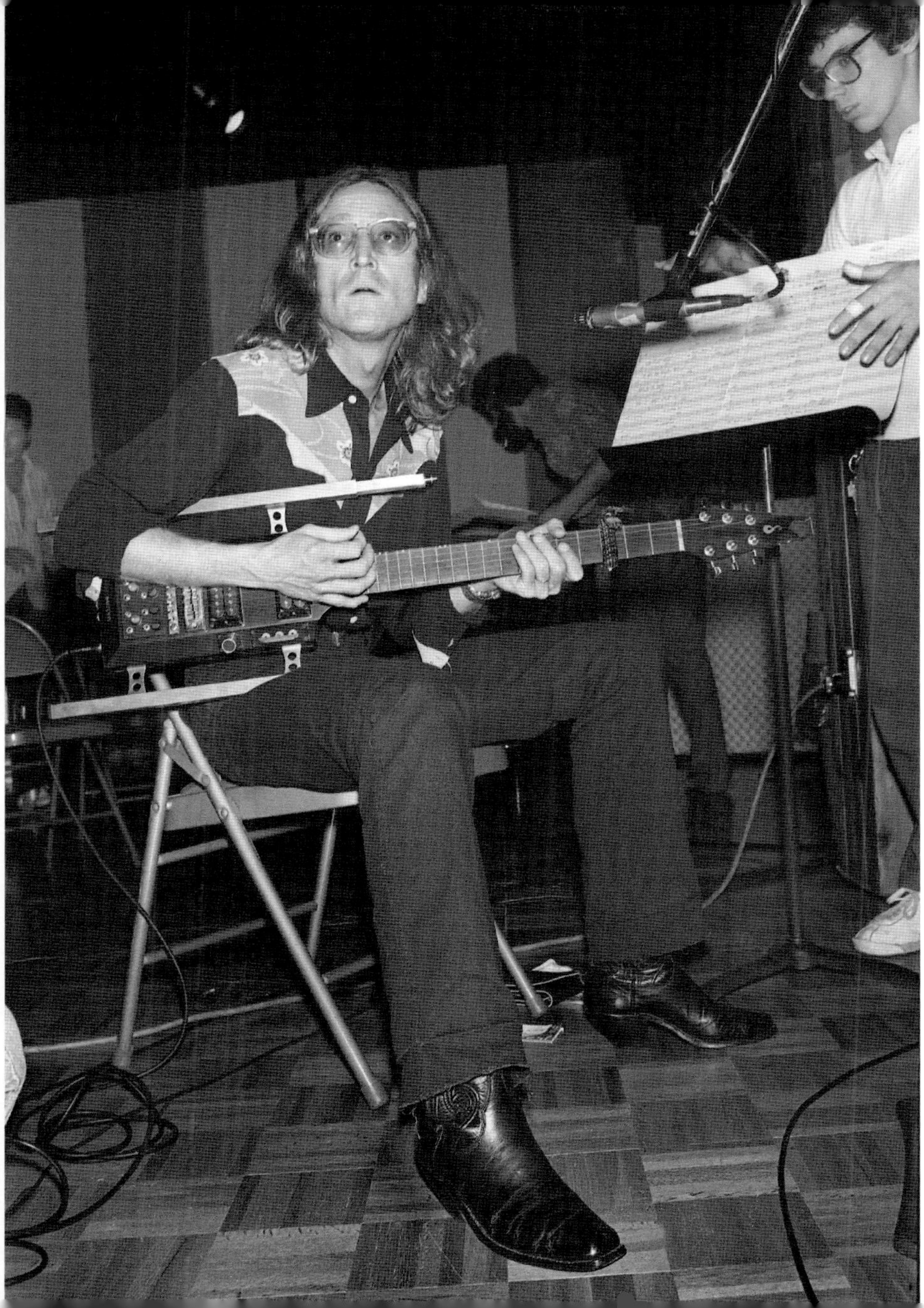

39. John and Yoko photo 26, August 7, 1980.

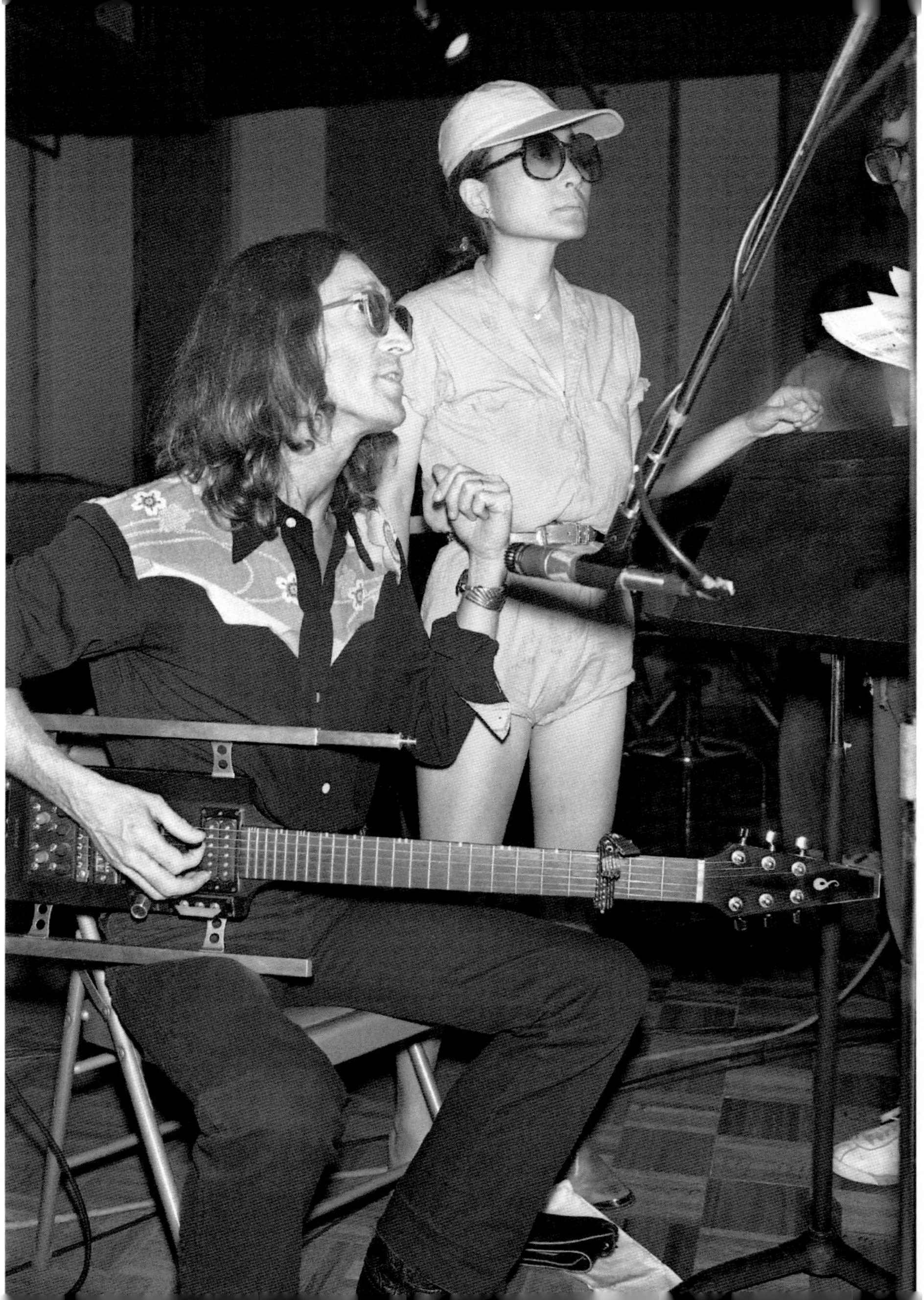

40. John and Yoko photo 27, August 7, 1980.

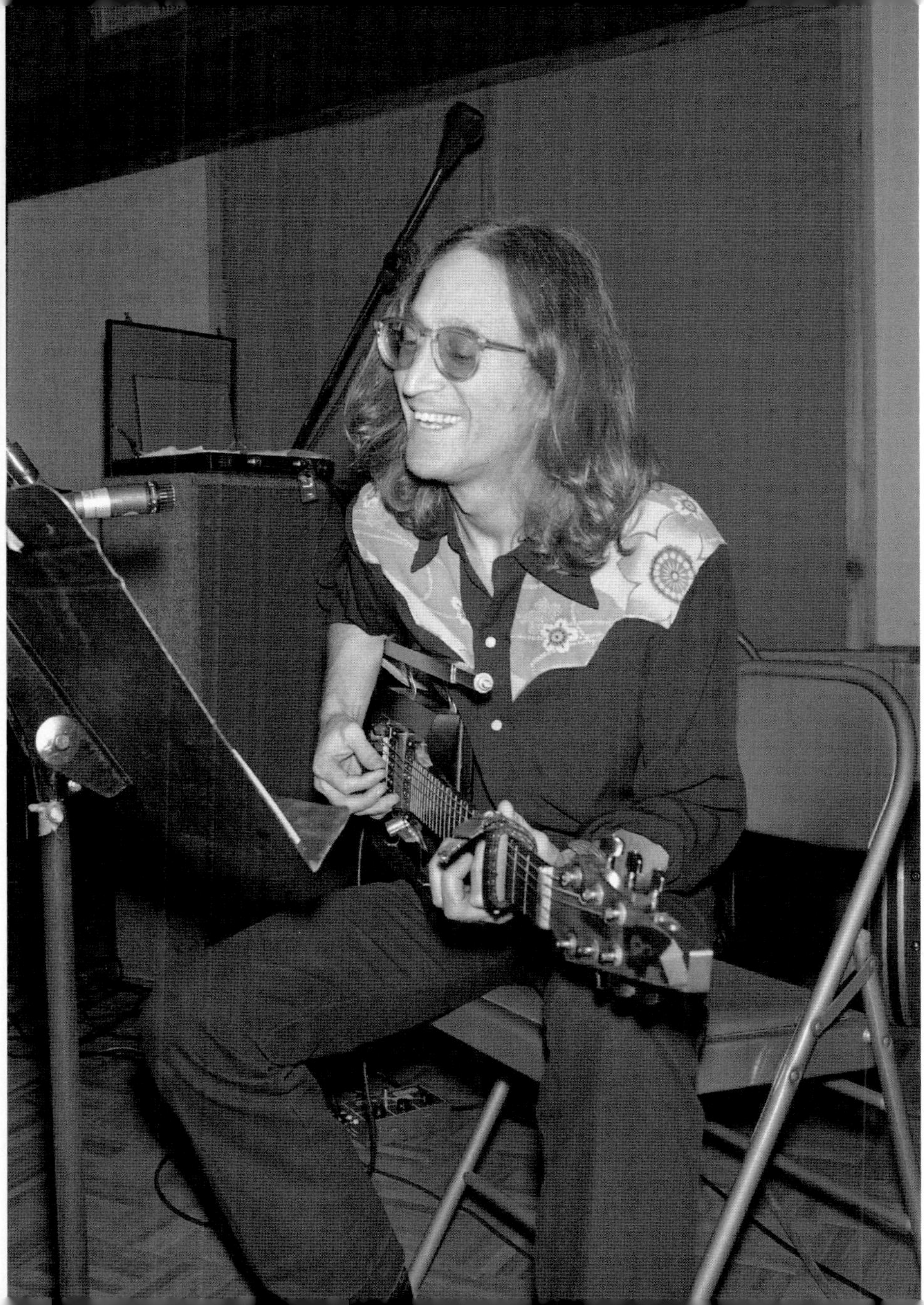

41. John and Yoko photo 28, August 7, 1980.

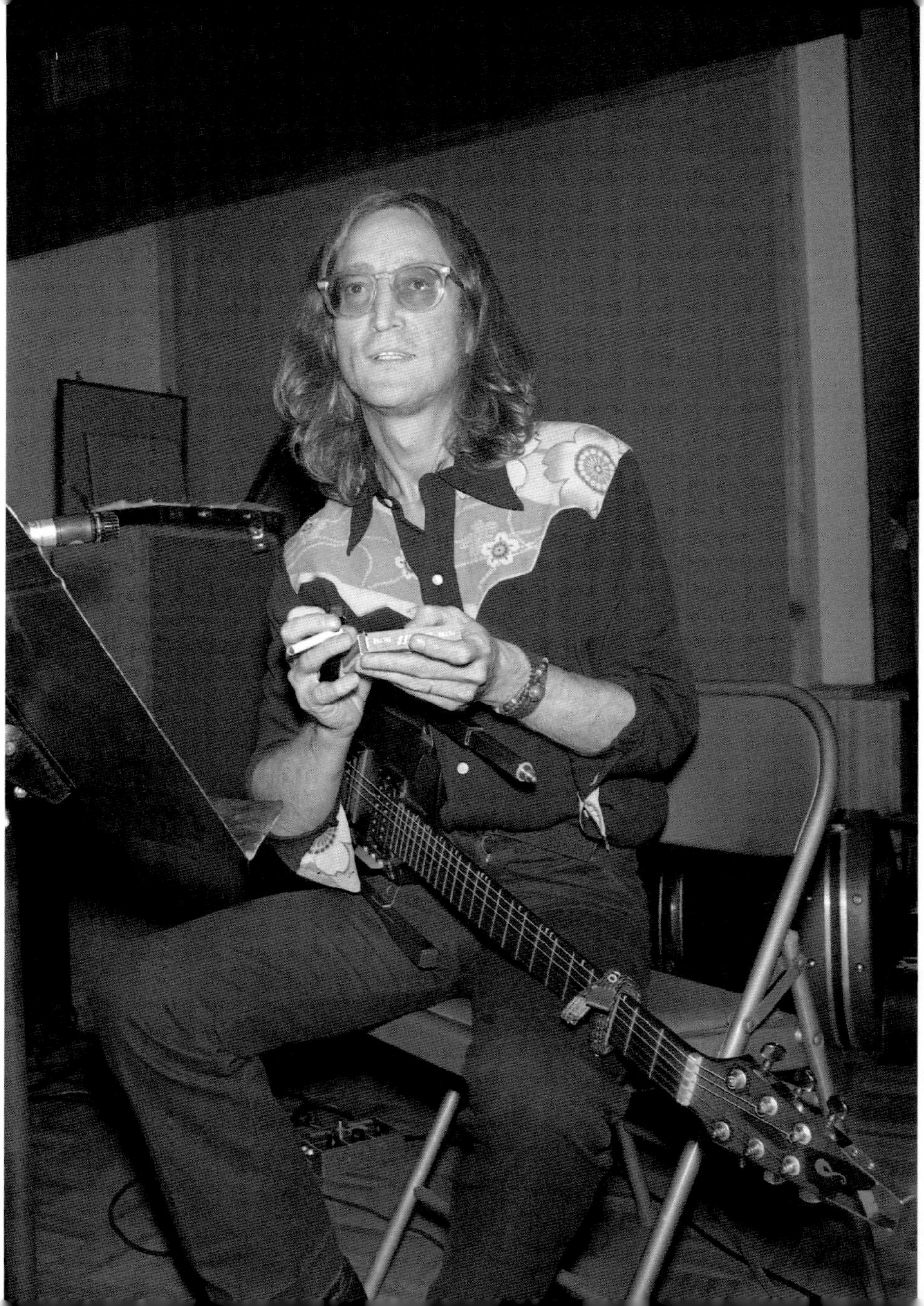

42. John and Yoko photo 29, August 7, 1980.

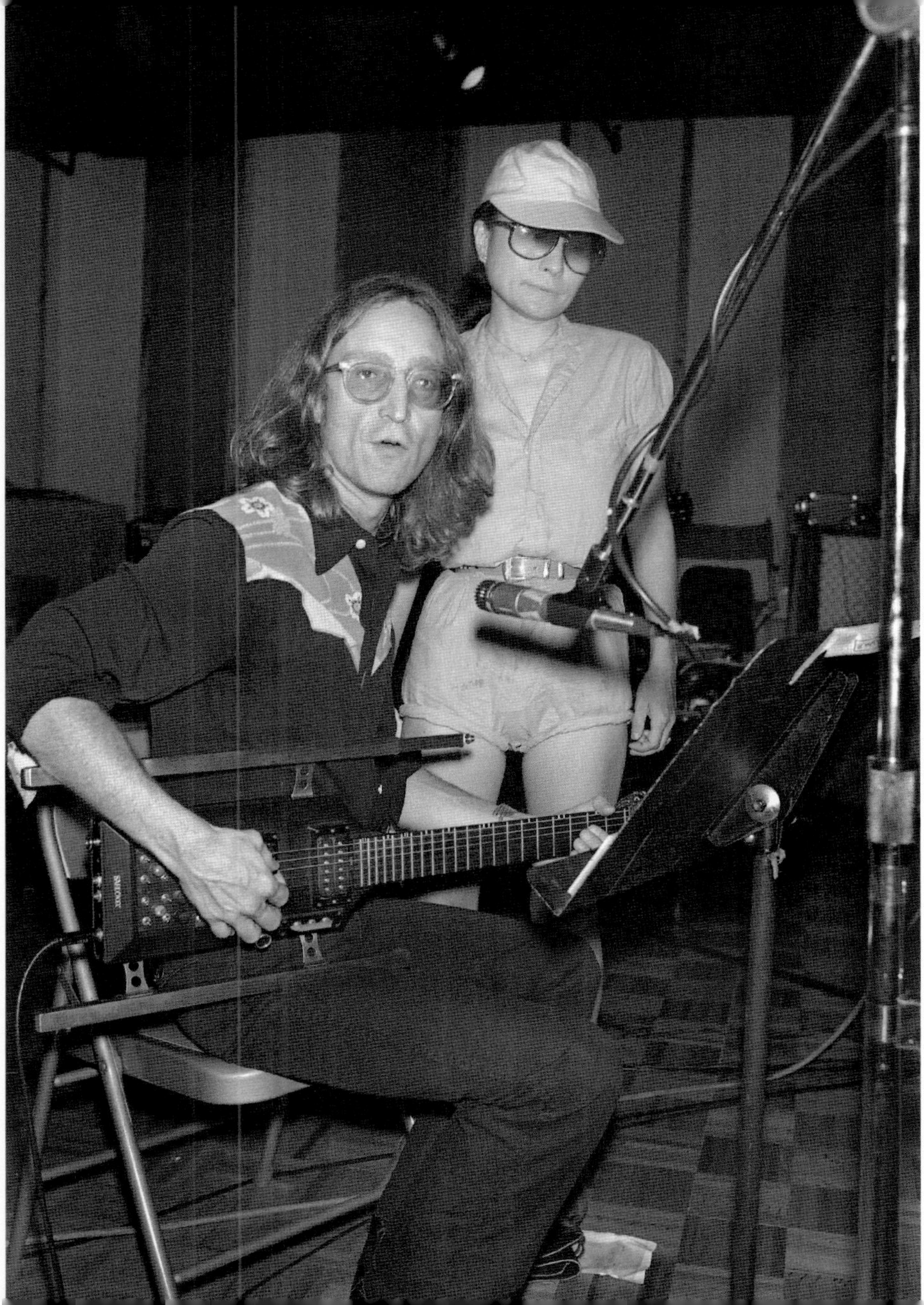

43. John and Yoko photo 30, August 7, 1980.

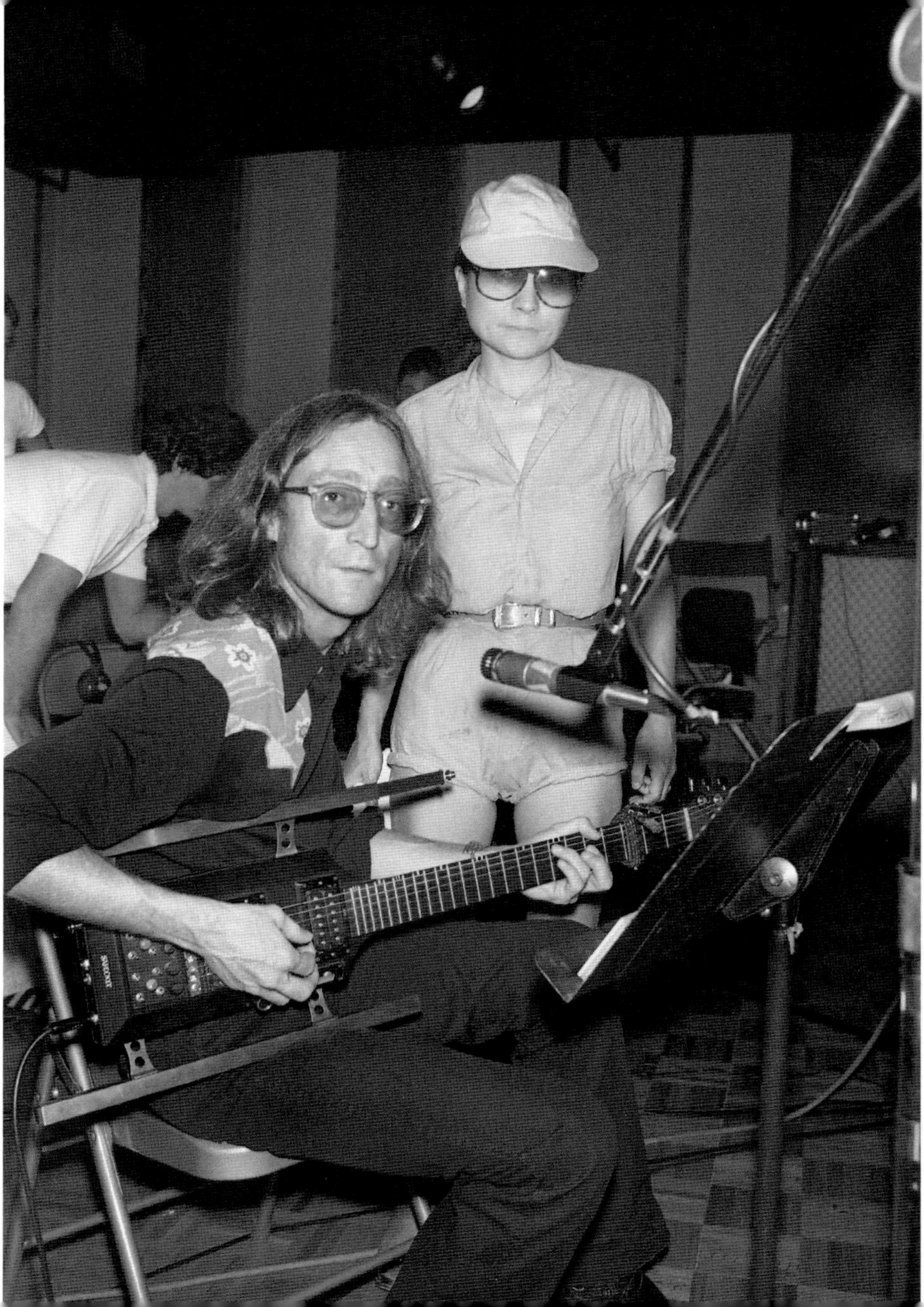

44. John and Yoko photo 31, August 7, 1980.

"May I ask you for one more photo with John before I head back?" Farrington said to Yoko. As if on cue, John began to strum the Sardonyx for the camera as Yoko posed herself in the frame to her husband's left. As a result, Farrington captured John off-guard as he turned to face the camera.

"I knew I had caught John awkwardly mid-expression," Farrington recalled, but the musicians were now gathering in earnest. "There was no question, this would be my final image."

As he tripped the shutter one more time, Farrington announced, "Last shot!" in an effort to reengage his subjects.

But the moment had clearly passed. Douglas was visible in the background, ready to gather the musicians for their first take. The photo session, for all intents and purposes, had ended. With a simple wave in the Lennons' direction, Farrington collected his equipment. "Thanks, Yoko," he said, as he made his way to the exit. "I'm heading back now and will have contacts ready for pickup by five."

Turning to face him, Yoko seemed finally to have ridden herself of the anxiety that had plagued her throughout the afternoon. Rather than scolding the photographer or providing some form of rebuke, she offered a gentle smile of approval. For Farrington, it made all the difference.

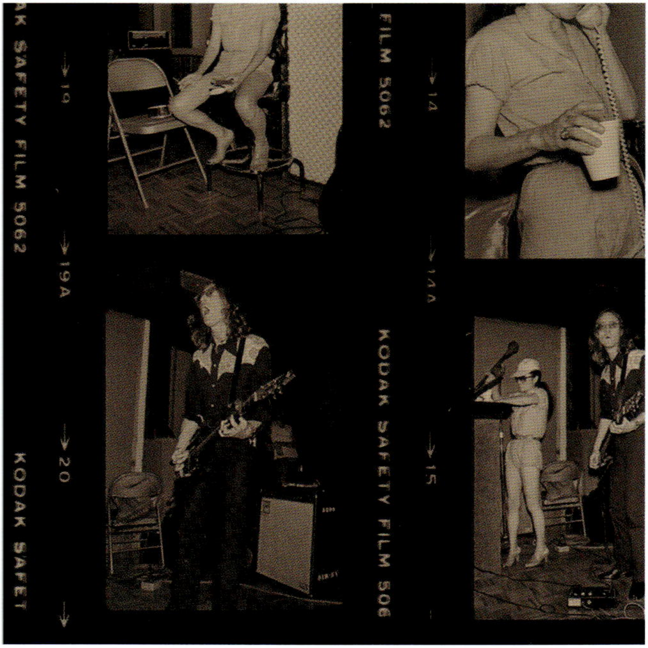

8.

Contact Sheet

As he left the Hit Factory that afternoon, Farrington's mission was ineluctably clear: airport, darkroom, deadline. Farrington may have alighted the studio in the company of John and Yoko, world-famous celebrities, but he was leaving all by his lonesome. As he traipsed through the studio, it seemed positively deserted in comparison to their nerve-racking arrival scarcely an hour earlier. But that was okay, he reasoned. "I had no expectations. Being on my own was part of the job description." So was breaking down and stowing his equipment in his trusty camera bag. All part of the ritual. Years later, he vividly recalled the moment in which he stepped back out into the afternoon sun on West 48th Street, exhausted yet eager to begin the next stage of this bizarre journey. Hailing a cab on nearby 10th Avenue, he felt a cathartic release as the summer heat continued to blanket the city.

In those pre-TSA days, travelers were able to negotiate their passage from check-in through departure with veritable ease. Farrington easily made the 3:00 P.M. shuttle from LaGuardia back to Boston. He made his way through the Logan Airport terminal on autopilot, marveling that his mission seemed to have been carried out in absolute secrecy. By 4:30 P.M., he had parked his bright red 1973 AMC Hornet hatchback outside his parents' home in Newton, where he kept a darkroom in the basement. Knowing that he would be on deadline, he had prepped the lab a few days earlier. The equipment was rudimentary and in working order, consisting of an enlarger, a bulb (and an extra bulb, for good measure), red safe-lights, thermometer, and timer. He had also rewashed all of his stainless-steel film-developing spools, along with his two- and four-spool developing tanks and their attendant black plastic lids in an effort to prevent any residual chemical contamination from previous jobs.

Farrington knew that he was entering a crucial stage of his work on behalf of the Lennons. As with breaking down his equipment, the routine of developing film was yet another step-by-step ritual when it came to professional photography during that era. The difference, however, between packing a camera bag and processing film was critical. One had to do multiple, sequential processing steps precisely, each and every time, so as not to completely destroy, or seriously damage, the delicate silver halide, negative emulsion. Without perfect negatives, one could not produce perfect prints from them. And he knew damn well that Yoko would be expecting perfection. "What I appreciated most about that tiny old basement space," he recalled, "was that all processing chemicals, stored in brown plastic gallon jugs in a plywood shelf above a line of four colored plastic 16 × 20 print-developing trays, were naturally maintained at a constant sixty-eight-degree temperature—even on the hottest of summer days."

With his equipment at the ready, Farrington got down to work. Let the ritual begin. First, he popped the cap off the plastic film canister, removing the film cassette and placing it upright on the wooden easel under his 4 × 5 Bessler enlarger. After tossing the canister, Larry Bird style, into the trash, he grabbed a pair of scissors and a metal bottle opener off the shelf, along with one double-reel developing tank with lid and cap, and two 35-mm manual film-loading reels. Having cordoned off his "dry" area, he prepared a corresponding "wet" area next to the trays and the sink. In those days, he recalled, "I used a standard lineup of Kodak black-and-white film developing chemicals: D-76 developer (with replenisher), acetic acid Stop Bath, standard Hypo Fixer, and a new, time-saving washing agent called PermaWash."

Thankfully, Farrington only had to process a single roll of film. He would need only eight ounces of each chemical, at proper concentration, to cover the film and reel inside the tank. But with the sixteen-ounce tank only half full of liquid, he would have to place the extra (unused) reel on top of the loaded reel to maintain proper chemical agitation and even development. From the four well-marked gallon jugs, he filled four smaller and individually labeled clear-plastic lab beakers, with measured amounts into each appropriate vessel. After confirming the correct order of his chemical lineup, he consulted his long, mercury thermometer and confirmed each at exactly 68°F. As the sharp, familiar scent of acetic acid and hyposulfite filled the darkroom, he switched on the nearby vent fan. With both his "wet" and "dry" areas ready and operational, he reached above the sink and, with a clicking sound, advanced the minute-hand on his oversized black GraLab timer to the seven-minute mark.

Working with full concentration D-76, Farrington's developing time would be a swift seven minutes, with ten seconds of careful tank-inversion agitation per minute. In those predigital days, it made for a remarkably swift production; by today's standards, it would be unbearably slow. After firmly closing the door and flicking off the overhead light, it took a moment for his eyes to adjust to total darkness and register zero light leaks that could damage the film during the loading process. Working in total darkness, he found the cassette and bottle opener, quickly snapped off the end cap (not unlike opening a beer), and slid the precious tightly rolled spool of film into his left palm. As the cap and empty cassette clinked on the darkroom floor, his right hand located the scissors while he used his left thumb to push up the film leader.

For Farrington, the next step was crucial, never failing to trigger memories of his Photography 101 course back in his college days. "What you are about to do next," his instructor had warned the class under the cloak of total darkness, "is probably the hardest thing you will ever have to learn to do in this class." First, one had to relax and understand that the inside width of the loading reel was slightly narrower than the width of 35-mm film. Hence, one had to carefully bend a slight arc between thumb and index finger before pushing the film inside the reel. But that was not the difficult part: the squared-off tag end had to be extended several inches, inserted into the reel, fitted into a center slot, and (depending on the make of the reel) either clipped under a tight spring or impaled on a sharp point. While keeping the film perfectly straight, he knew he had to maintain a smooth winding motion to properly load the film onto the reel. With the emulsion side down, the film had to be spooled accordingly so that the chemicals would flow evenly through and around every square inch of the film.

Farrington knew that any false move could result in total disaster and the loss of the precious images that he had captured back in New York City. Placing the reel into the tank along with the extra unloaded reel on top, he firmly pressed down onto the light-proof plastic lid. Switching the light back on, he watched the second hand begin its counterclockwise, seven-minute countdown. Flipping the pouring cap off and tilting the tank toward his right-handed beaker of D-76, he poured the negative developer rapidly into the light-tight container without spilling a drop. Giving the tank three gentle inversions and tapping it three times against the sink edge (to release any air bubbles clinging to the emulsion), he placed it gently on the counter. Precisely at the seven-minute mark, Farrington drained the developer and immediately poured the Stop Bath solution into the tank, giving it one minute of continuous, gentle agitation. Next, it was finally time to "fix" the latent images with six minutes of fresh fixer, agitated gently every minute for ten seconds. After that, all that was required for archival permanence was a one-minute water rinse, one-minute PermaWash, and a second one-minute water rinse.

By this point, Farrington's anticipation was reaching a fever pitch. Removing the reels from the tank, he turned to the darkroom's bright overhead light, held the dripping reel upward, and began to gently unspool the wet film off the reel. The moment of truth had arrived. He felt a deep sense of relief as the individual images slowly wound off the reel. With the light playing off them, John and Yoko came fully into view. For the most part, the negatives looked good, although the contrast—with its bright sun and deep shadows—troubled him. "Better to be slightly overexposed than under," he concluded, scanning the first series of images at arm's length in front of the light. There they were: his last photos of John and Yoko at the studio. Unwinding a few more feet of film, he caught sight of John and Yoko entering the Hit Factory. "Two decent publicity shots," he thought to himself. Mission accomplished.

Farrington was almost there. Adding a small amount of wetting agent to the water prior to drying the film was critical in preventing droplets from leaving hard-to-remove water marks and stains that would end up on the prints. Gently removing the reel from the tank and carrying it over to the darkroom's drying cabinet, Farrington clipped the film's end onto a suspended wooden clothespin, slowly unwinding the film until it came loose from its reel and finally—*finally*—attaching a weighted clip to the film's bottom. As the wetting agent shed water from the newly developed film, he could tell that his negatives were nigh-on perfect—one side clean and glossy, while the other side revealed a dull emulsion. Shutting the cabinet door to prevent dust intrusion, he used an old hair dryer to dry out the negatives. "Time to call Charles Cohen," he announced, staring at the humming cabinet. The contact sheets would be ready in half an hour. It was the usual drill, just another completed job ready to go out the door on deadline.

But in truth, Farrington knew that there was nothing rote about this assignment. Not surprisingly, Cohen answered on the first ring. "Do you have any photos ready for me yet?" he asked, feigning impatience. "You can pick up the contact sheet in half an hour," Farrington replied. But why had Cohen said "photos"? Farrington knew full well that his same-day job description *specified* only contact sheets. At this juncture, prints wouldn't need to be prepared unless there had been a leak to the press, and from what the photographer could tell, the top-secret shoot had gone off without a hitch.

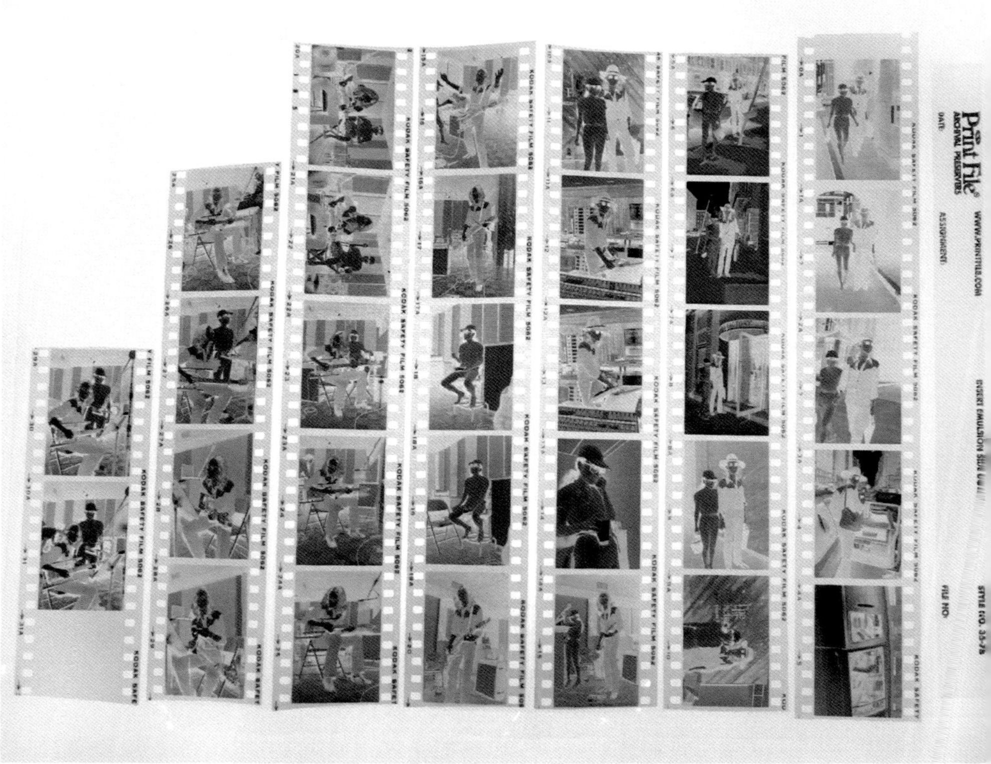

45. John and Yoko negatives, August 7, 1980.

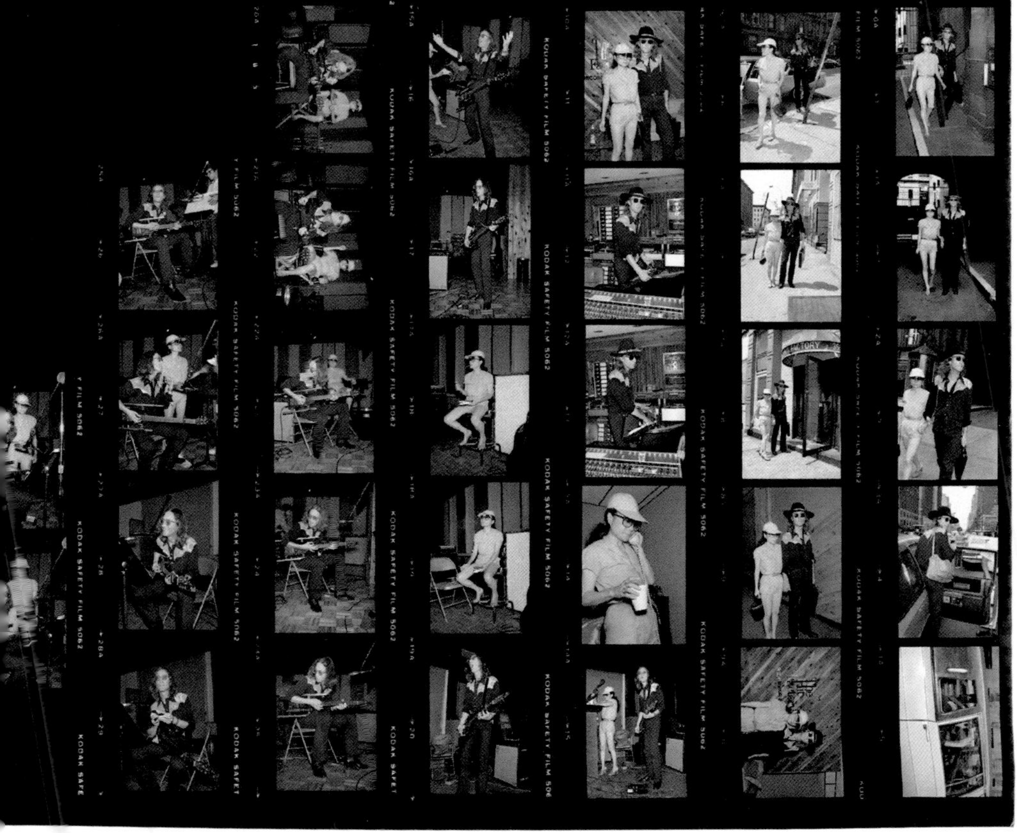

16. John and Yoko contact sheet, August 8, 1980.

Cohen didn't mince any words. "You can forget about the contact sheet," he retorted. "How soon can you get me two complete sets of 8 × 10 prints? Yoko wants you to make one 8 × 10 print of each shot you took with numbers on the back. And you can make a set for me, too," he added. Before Farrington could get a word in edgewise, Cohen continued barking out orders. "She wants to have two sets made so that we can make the final selection. How soon can you have them ready?" To Farrington's mind, this was untenable. With such a high-profile client, there was simply no way he could take the negatives over to Jet Photo lab and pay super-rush charges for sixty-two prints. John and Yoko's photos would have to be custom prints, Farrington protested, in order to maintain abject secrecy. Cohen had no option but to demur. "I have to send Yoko's prints out tomorrow afternoon," he replied, confirming Farrington's new deadline. "And don't forget to include your total bill—for everything—and charge Yoko for the rush job. She's not worried about it." He laughed as he hung up the receiver.

As promised, Farrington delivered the prints to Cohen's Back Bay offices promptly at 3:00 P.M. the next day. Oddly, Cohen was not in evidence. Usually, he was there to greet Farrington and celebrate a job well done. Instead, Cohen's receptionist quietly took possession of the precious cargo, which was messengered by private limo to Yoko's Studio One office at the Dakota. The photographer dutifully calculated his invoice:

Standard day rate:	$250.00
Rush-job surcharge:	$50.00
Film processing and contact sheets:	$8.50
Two sets of 8 × 10 glossy proofs:	$124.00
Eastern Airlines shuttle expenses:	$59.90
Taxi fare:	$24.00
Sales tax (5%):	$21.63
Total:	$538.03

For the photographer, the whole business felt strangely deflating. "I hardly expected a champagne cork-popping welcome," Farrington later reflected, "but I certainly expected for Cohen to be waiting." He had just concluded the most important job of his career—of *both* of their careers—and Cohen was nowhere in sight. No, it was an odd reception to say the least.

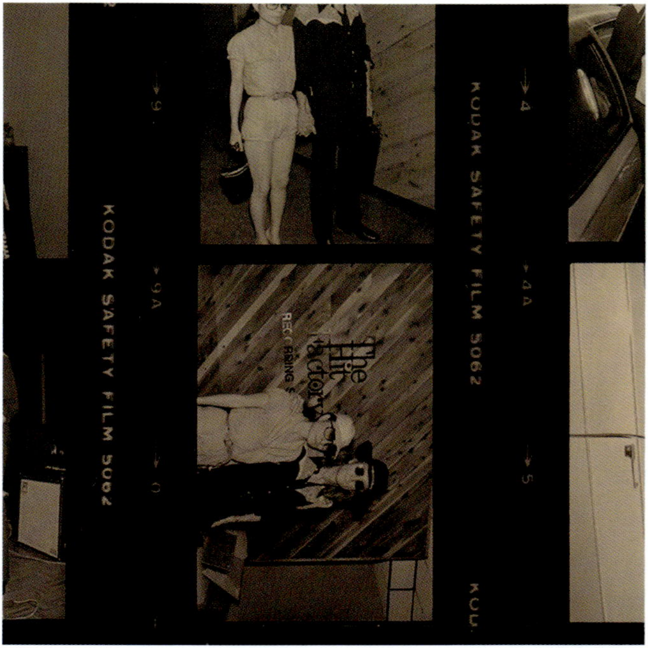
KODAK SAFETY FILM 5062
KODAK SAFETY FILM 5062
The Hit Factory

9.

Press Release

As the hours ticked by across the long weekend after Farrington left Cohen's offices, his anxiety understandably got the best of him. He began to doubt that his photographs would even be used. "Had Yoko brought in another photographer after I left?" he wondered. "Were new images already being generated and selected?" Perhaps if he had stayed overnight—as Yoko herself had suggested—Farrington might have been able to shoot the actual recording sessions, gathering even more images in the process. But that wasn't his assignment, he reminded himself. As Saturday shifted into Sunday, the wires remained ever quiet when it came to news about John and Yoko's activities at the Hit Factory. The top-secret mission seemed to have been a stark-raving success. Nobody was the wiser.

As it turned out, Farrington didn't have to wait very long. Plan B had apparently won the day. Amazingly, the Big Secret had remained intact. By the time that Tuesday, August 12, rolled around, the coast was clear, and Cohen was able to deliver his carefully crafted press release, tantalizingly headlined as "Love Fantasy Theme Highlights New John Lennon and Yoko Ono Album," to an unsuspecting world. As Farrington had predicted, Yoko and the publicity agent had selected the photo of the Lennons standing below the awning of the Hit Factory's 48th Street entrance. United Press International carried the press release, which announced that "former Beatle John Lennon and his wife, Yoko Ono, are emerging as recording artists again, according to a source close to the internationally famous, fabulously wealthy couple." In addition to reporting that "a label has not yet been selected," but "a release date is set for early fall," the statement added that "the musicians are all excited over the new Lennon material," which "is the best of Lennon to date."[1] Farrington could easily discern Cohen's penchant for hype all over the press release. The hyperbole was simply incredible. An unnamed "source." Really?

In short order, Cohen's press release—and Farrington's photo—began appearing in newspapers and magazines across the globe. A few days later, the photographer telephoned Cohen's offices for an update. The PR man's account executive Bruce Replogle took the call. "Yoko chose the shot you liked. You called it," he reported. For his part, Farrington was eager to learn what had transpired after he departed the Hit Factory on Thursday. While Farrington busied himself with the contact sheets, Replogle had joined the Lennons in the studio. "It was so cool," Replogle continued, "John, Yoko, and the band were recording tracks, and I was just hanging out with them. The music is unbelievable," Bruce gushed excitedly. "I had lunch with them, too. It was amazing. Yoko ordered huge plates of sushi delivered to the studio during the break," he laughed. "Only a couple guys in the band would touch it. They secretly ordered cheeseburgers without Yoko catching on."

"Wow," Farrington replied. "You had a lot more fun than I did! We were all walking around on eggshells." The photographer couldn't help asking about how Ono had received his photos. "You got some amazing shots—John rocking that guitar is so cool—but Yoko's sending John out to a hair salon for a new '80s-looking haircut," he explained. "It's not your photos; it's his long, stringy hair that Yoko insisted had to go." In a burst of encouragement, Replogle added, "Your photo is running all over the world. Yoko and Charles are really happy with all the press

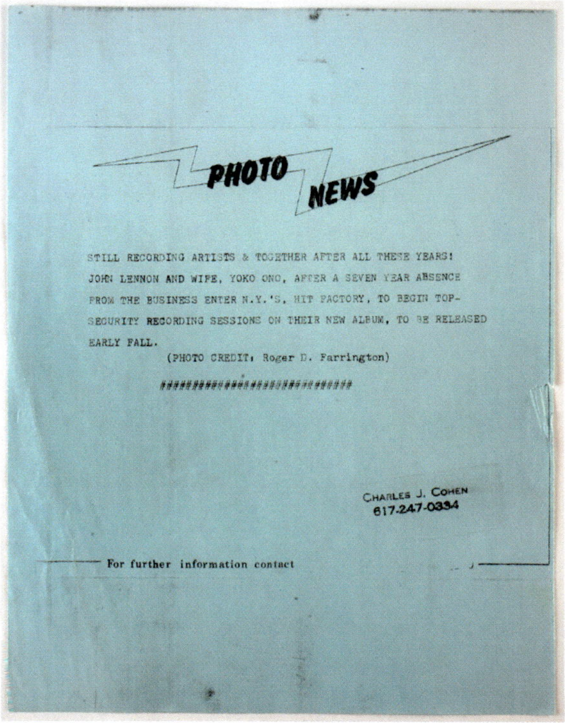

PHOTO NEWS

STILL RECORDING ARTISTS & TOGETHER AFTER ALL THESE YEARS!
JOHN LENNON AND WIFE, YOKO ONO, AFTER A SEVEN YEAR ABSENCE
FROM THE BUSINESS ENTER N.Y.'S, HIT FACTORY, TO BEGIN TOP-
SECURITY RECORDING SESSIONS ON THEIR NEW ALBUM, TO BE RELEASED
EARLY FALL.
(PHOTO CREDIT: Roger D. Farrington)

###############################

CHARLES J. COHEN
617-247-0334

For further information contact

47. Advertising and Entertainment transmittal page, August 12, 1980.

pouring in." It was certainly good news, Farrington had to admit. But at the same time, he knew intuitively that John's new look would require matching photos to be taken as soon as possible. It was an inevitable aspect of the PR process. His photos, the last official images of John letting his freak flag fly—his cowboy regalia in full flower at the Hit Factory on August 7, 1980—would shortly be relegated to the dustbin of music history.[2]

Apparently, Farrington's moment in the sun wasn't quite over just yet. It was perhaps a week later when Farrington received an unexpected

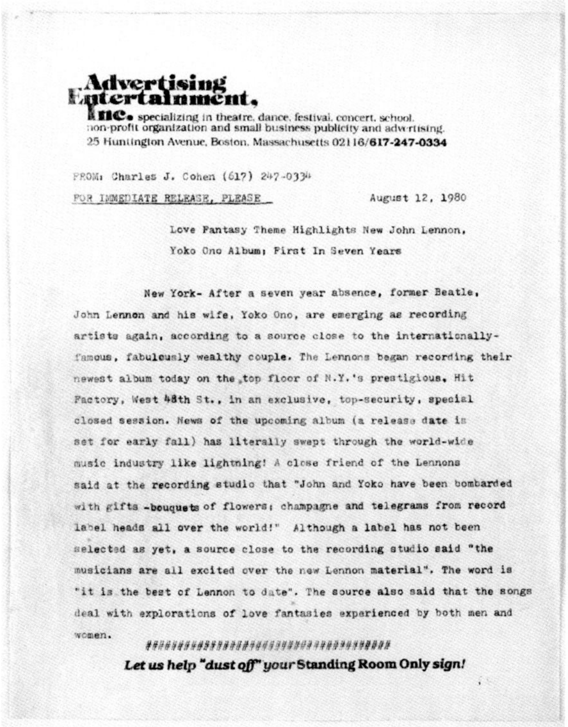

Advertising Entertainment, Inc. specializing in theatre, dance, festival, concert, school, non-profit organization and small business publicity and advertising.
25 Huntington Avenue, Boston, Massachusetts 02116/617-247-0334

FROM: Charles J. Cohen (617) 247-0334

FOR IMMEDIATE RELEASE, PLEASE   August 12, 1980

Love Fantasy Theme Highlights New John Lennon,
Yoko Ono Album; First In Seven Years

New York- After a seven year absence, former Beatle, John Lennon and his wife, Yoko Ono, are emerging as recording artists again, according to a source close to the internationally-famous, fabulously wealthy couple. The Lennons began recording their newest album today on the top floor of N.Y.'s prestigious, Hit Factory, West 48th St., in an exclusive, top-security, special closed session. News of the upcoming album (a release date is set for early fall) has literally swept through the world-wide music industry like lightning! A close friend of the Lennons said at the recording studio that "John and Yoko have been bombarded with gifts -bouquets of flowers; champagne and telegrams from record label heads all over the world!" Although a label has not been selected as yet, a source close to the recording studio said "the musicians are all excited over the new Lennon material". The word is "it is the best of Lennon to date". The source also said that the songs deal with explorations of love fantasies experienced by both men and women.

################################

Let us help "dust off" your **Standing Room Only** *sign!*

48. Advertising and Entertainment press release, August 12, 1980.

telephone call from *Rolling Stone* magazine's Ben Fong-Torres. "Am I speaking to the photographer who was in the recording studio with John Lennon?" he asked. Farrington was caught off-guard. The voice sounded too professional to be one of his friends pulling his leg. "We don't want to use the standard publicity photo from the agency," Fong-Torres continued. "Do you have any others? We'd like to buy another photo you took of John Lennon in the studio. Our readers would be eager to hear from someone who was there. It's for our 'Random Notes' column." Any misgivings Farrington might have had suddenly vanished. This was clearly a once-in-a-lifetime opportunity to be quoted in *Rolling Stone* magazine—and about John Lennon recording a new album, no less. "We can pay you for a different photo," Fong-Torres added. "Do you have one of *just John*?" There it was, Farrington thought. He could already feel the anxiety roiling inside of him. His instructions from Cohen had been explicit when it came to photographing John and Yoko together as a package deal.

In retrospect, it all made sense to Farrington. *Rolling Stone* was rock 'n' roll's monthly bible, with an enormous circulation and editorial clout, to boot. But the magazine's tough, egotistical publisher, Jann Wenner, was in a long-running feud with Ono. Farrington was suddenly in the distressing position of having to negotiate between Cohen's dictum and the opportunity to have his work published in *Rolling Stone.* The biggest rock 'n' roll story in the past five years is breaking worldwide, and Farrington found himself in the ignominious position, however fortuitous, of being the photographer who was there.

Farrington sensed an even deeper issue at the heart of the matter: Had Cohen and Replogle, under pressure perhaps from Yoko, declined to give Wenner what he wanted? To his credit, the photographer opted to play it straight. Taking a deep breath, he finally delivered his reply to Fong-Torres, pointing out that "I have other photos, including John playing the guitar, but whatever shot I give you will have to include Yoko." Recognizing that this may be a deal-breaker for the magazine, he added, "My assignment was to photograph both of them together." Farrington sensed that Fong-Torres was listening intently. "But I have to call the agency to confirm," he concluded. If there was a deal to be made, Farrington told Fong-Torres, "you can pay me your standard single-usage rate."

This might work out, after all. Perhaps there was a way for Farrington to have his cake and eat it, too. The photographer shortly came to realize that his position wasn't as tentative as he first imagined. He wondered why Cohen's office hadn't called him about the magazine's photo request. *Rolling Stone* undoubtedly knew about Advertising & Entertainment's role in the matter. The name of Cohen's agency was plastered all over the press release. Cohen's office had thirty additional proof prints at their disposal. And that's when it hit him: Advertising & Entertainment didn't hold the exclusive rights to Farrington's August 7, 1980, photographs. They had deployed the selected image for purposes of the press release and now they needed Farrington's permission to use any of the others. Whether Cohen's firm liked it or not, Farrington had the express right to license his images directly to any and all interested parties.

A telephone call to Replogle confirmed what Farrington already knew. *Rolling Stone* had been in touch with Cohen's firm and ascertained that they had to deal with the photographer if they wanted any additional images. "It's cool," the account exec explained. "They just want to buy another photo from you, and I gave them lots of exclusive information already from when I was in the studio during the recording session." And besides, Replogle added, somewhat dismissively, "it's just a small item for 'Random Notes' in the September issue." Sensing an opening, Farrington noted that Fong-Torres wanted a solo shot of John. "I don't want to piss off Yoko," he said, "but I bet they'd love the shot of John playing with the mic." When Replogle didn't bite, Farrington tried another tack. "But I'm thinking the best two-shot is the one with John looking up while playing, with Yoko smoking and gazing in his direction." Farrington would play by Cohen and Yoko's rules—*for now*.

After accepting *Rolling Stone*'s standard $75 rate, Farrington sent the photo to Fong-Torres. When the magazine's September 18 issue hit the newsstands, he proudly purchased a copy and thumbed his way to "Random Notes," where he caught sight of his photo of John and Yoko, who were prominently featured above the words, "John Lennon has ended his five-year recording moratorium."[3] Farrington was duly pleased with the photo's presentation. "It looked cool and candid," he recalled, "just what my assignment had called for." He was somewhat disappointed that the image of John's striking black Sardonyx guitar body had been lost against his black shirt.

Even still, Farrington admired the manner in which the magazine's photo editors had removed the top portion of the original photograph's dark background. In those days, it was a time-consuming, nondigital process by which a "mask" was created by carefully outlining the subjects while removing the background. The technique packed plenty of visual punch, rendering the photo even more impactful. "It was an excellent, broad-brush, sweeping item," Farrington had to admit, "extremely well done. I felt good about having a hand in the story's impact and believed that my photo had a classic look, hearkening back to the Beatles' twilight years when an aloof Yoko sat next to John as he strummed his famous Epiphone Casino at Abbey Road."

Farrington enjoyed the fanfare that the "Random Notes" photo generated. As word began to spread that he had been the photographer of record in the studio with John and Yoko, he received several phone calls from mostly curious and excitable friends, colleagues, and even a couple of well-known Boston-area musicians. "Huge Beatles fans, one and all," he recalled, "they were mostly interested in my firsthand stories about hanging out with the great Lennon. Within a few weeks, interest had dissipated and not having to answer questions about my 'Lennon shoot' was a welcome relief." Farrington's professional colleagues understood that it had been a tough shoot, and coming away with a few usable photos had been a coup under the circumstances.

In those days, blockbuster news stories along the lines of John and Yoko's return to the studio broke far and wide through hundreds of print publications over the course of several weeks. "It's hard to believe how instant and unceasing news stories are today in comparison to 1980," Farrington points out. "It's even harder to consider that some of the highest circulation weekly or monthly magazines took weeks—sometimes more than a month—to publish a story." In the aforementioned example vis-à-vis "Random Notes," *Rolling Stone* licensed Farrington's photo in mid-August for an issue that wouldn't be published until mid-September, more than a month later. As autumn proceeded, and the Lennons

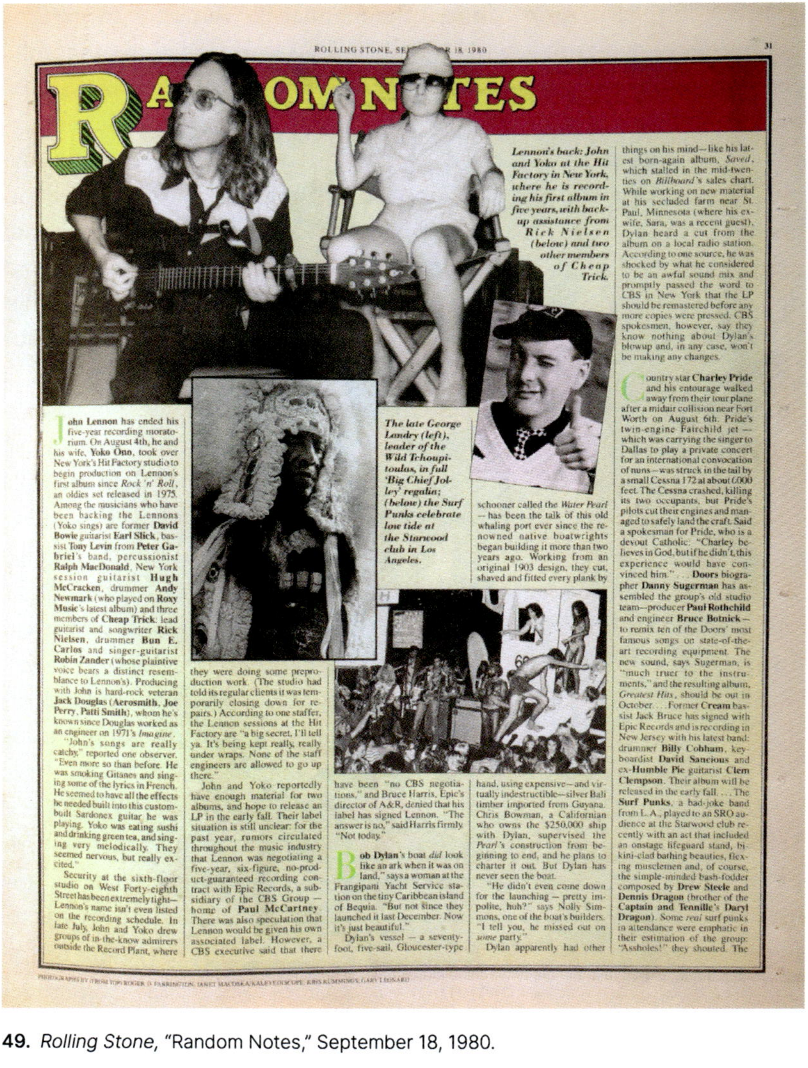

ROLLING STONE, SE…R 18, 1980 31

RANDOM NOTES

Lennon's back: John and Yoko at the Hit Factory in New York, where he is recording his first album in five years, with backup assistance from Rick Nielsen (below) and two other members of Cheap Trick.

The late George Landry (left), leader of the Wild Tchoupitoulas, in full 'Big Chief Jolley' regalia; (below) the Surf Punks celebrate low tide at the Starwood club in Los Angeles.

John Lennon has ended his five-year recording moratorium. On August 4th, he and his wife, **Yoko Ono**, took over New York's Hit Factory studio to begin production on Lennon's first album since *Rock 'n' Roll*, an oldies set released in 1975. Among the musicians who have been backing the Lennons (Yoko sings) are former **David Bowie** guitarist **Earl Slick**, bassist **Tony Levin** from **Peter Gabriel**'s band, percussionist **Ralph MacDonald**, New York session guitarist **Hugh McCracken**, drummer **Andy Newmark** (who played on **Roxy Music**'s latest album) and three members of **Cheap Trick**: lead guitarist and songwriter **Rick Nielsen**, drummer **Bun E. Carlos** and singer-guitarist **Robin Zander** (whose plaintive voice bears a distinct resemblance to Lennon's). Producing with John is hard-rock veteran **Jack Douglas** (**Aerosmith**, **Joe Perry**, **Patti Smith**), whom he's known since Douglas worked as an engineer on 1971's *Imagine*.

"John's songs are really catchy," reported one observer. "Even more so than before. He was smoking Gitanes and singing some of the lyrics in French. He seemed to have all the effects he needed built into this custom-built Sardonex guitar he was playing. Yoko was eating sushi and drinking green tea, and singing very melodically. They seemed nervous, but really excited."

Security at the sixth-floor studio on West Forty-eighth Street has been extremely tight—Lennon's name isn't even listed on the recording schedule. In late July, John and Yoko drew groups of in-the-know admirers outside the Record Plant, where they were doing some preproduction work. (The studio had told its regular clients it was temporarily closing down for repairs.) According to one staffer, the Lennon sessions at the Hit Factory are "a big secret, I'll tell ya. It's being kept really, really under wraps. None of the staff engineers are allowed to go up there."

John and Yoko reportedly have enough material for two albums, and hope to release an LP in the early fall. Their label situation is still unclear: for the past year, rumors circulated throughout the music industry that Lennon was negotiating a five-year, six-figure, no-product-guaranteed recording contract with Epic Records, a subsidiary of the CBS Group — home of **Paul McCartney**. There was also speculation that Lennon would be given his own associated label. However, a CBS executive said that there have been "no CBS negotiations," and Bruce Harris, Epic's director of A&R, denied that his label has signed Lennon. "The answer is no," said Harris firmly. "Not today."

Bob Dylan's boat *did* look like an ark when it was on land," says a woman at the Frangipani Yacht Service station on the tiny Caribbean island of Bequia. "But not since they launched it last December. Now it's just beautiful."

Dylan's vessel — a seventy-foot, five-sail, Gloucester-type schooner called the *Water Pearl* — has been the talk of this old whaling port ever since the renowned native boatwrights began building it more than two years ago. Working from an original 1903 design, they cut, shaved and fitted every plank by hand, using expensive—and virtually indestructible—silver Bali timber imported from Guyana. Chris Bowman, a Californian who owns the $250,000 ship with Dylan, supervised the *Pearl*'s construction from beginning to end, and he plans to charter it out. But Dylan has never seen the boat.

"He didn't even come down for the launching — pretty impolite, huh?" says Nolly Simmons, one of the boat's builders. "I tell you, he missed out on *some* party."

Dylan apparently had other things on his mind—like his latest born-again album, *Saved*, which stalled in the mid-twenties on *Billboard*'s sales chart. While working on new material at his secluded farm near St. Paul, Minnesota (where his ex-wife, Sara, was a recent guest), Dylan heard a cut from the album on a local radio station. According to one source, he was shocked by what he considered to be an awful sound mix and promptly passed the word to CBS in New York that the LP should be remastered before any more copies were pressed. CBS spokesmen, however, say they know nothing about Dylan's blowup and, in any case, won't be making any changes.

Country star **Charley Pride** and his entourage walked away from their tour plane after a midair collision near Fort Worth on August 6th. Pride's twin-engine Fairchild jet — which was carrying the singer to Dallas to play a private concert for an international convocation of nuns—was struck in the tail by a small Cessna 172 at about 6000 feet. The Cessna crashed, killing its two occupants, but Pride's pilots cut their engines and managed to safely land the craft. Said a spokesman for Pride, who is a devout Catholic: "Charley believes in God, but if he didn't, this experience would have convinced him." . . . **Doors** biographer **Danny Sugerman** has assembled the group's old studio team—producer **Paul Rothchild** and engineer **Bruce Botnick** — to remix ten of the Doors' most famous songs on state-of-the-art recording equipment. The new sound, says Sugerman, is "much truer to the instruments," and the resulting album, *Greatest Hits*, should be out in October. . . . Former **Cream** bassist Jack Bruce has signed with Epic Records and is recording in New Jersey with his latest band: drummer **Billy Cobham**, keyboardist **David Sancious** and ex-**Humble Pie** guitarist **Clem Clempson**. Their album will be released in the early fall. . . . The **Surf Punks**, a bad-joke band from L.A., played to an SRO audience at the Starwood club recently with an act that included an onstage lifeguard stand, bikini-clad bathing beauties, flexing musclemen and, of course, the simple-minded bash-fodder composed by **Drew Steele** and **Dennis Dragon** (brother of the **Captain and Tennille**'s **Daryl Dragon**). Some *real* surf punks in attendance were emphatic in their estimation of the group: "Assholes!" they shouted. The

PHOTOGRAPHS BY (FROM TOP) ROGER D. FARRINGTON; JANET MACOSKA/KALEIDOSCOPE; KRIS KUMMINGS; GARY LEONARD

49. *Rolling Stone*, "Random Notes," September 18, 1980.

prepared for the bravura release of their *Double Fantasy* LP in November, Farrington began to realize that "handing over thirty-one 8 × 10 'numbered proofs' to Cohen had been a mistake. He had sent them out at least two or three times without my permission and/or compensation and—as this was not Cohen's first misuse of my Lennon photos—I had to ask him firmly to cease with the unauthorized giveaways."

Things came to a head when Cohen authorized Boston's *Musician's Magazine* to publish one of Farrington's photos of Lennon playing his Sardonyx at the Hit Factory as its inaugural cover photo. "Cohen's apology was lame," Farrington recalled. The PR flak explained that "they're a tiny new local publication. I was trying to help them out." And besides, Cohen added dismissively, "you got a nice photo credit. I didn't think you'd mind, and maybe they'll give you some work." Farrington didn't give up so easily, reminding Cohen about the fracas with *Rolling Stone*. Knowing that the photographer was legally and ethically in the right, Cohen worked another angle: "Your photos are running in papers and magazines around the world," he countered. "You should be thanking me, not bitching to me about some local rag. The clippings have been pouring in, and the press book we're putting together for Yoko is huge. You should see it!" he exclaimed. Anyway, "you should stop complaining," he concluded, "or you won't get any more work from me."

As far as Cohen was concerned, the gauntlet had been thrown. But he was right about one thing: the effects of Farrington's Hit Factory photographs could be felt far and wide. For one thing, music lovers quickly ascertained that it was eminently possible to see John and Yoko in their natural habitat. As a result, the crowds in front of the Dakota grew precipitously larger. *Everybody* wanted a glimpse of the famous couple, and Farrington's photographs were proof positive that it was possible to see a Beatle in the flesh on the streets of New York City. But the effects of Farrington's photographs didn't end there.

Cohen's press release, and its attendant image of John and Yoko entering the Hit Factory, captured the attention of David Geffen, the maverick music executive who had founded his new eponymous record label. "I knew it would be quite a coup to sign them, but I didn't think I had a chance," Geffen recalled. "I wrote Yoko a letter—because I knew that the only person who could make it happen was her. John had complete faith in her; he trusted her in all decisions about business. His motive in recording *Double Fantasy* was completely romantic in that he wanted the record to show the world Yoko's talents and for his wife to finally get the recognition he felt she deserved. He wanted the light to shine on her." After running his astrological numbers, Yoko inked the *Double Fantasy* deal with Geffen in exchange for a fifty-fifty split of the profits.[4] The Holstein cows, it turned out, were a mere entrée when it came to Yoko's deal-making abilities.

Cohen's hyped-up press release also caught the attention of writer Laurence Shames, who authored a November 1 *Esquire* cover story titled, "John Lennon, Where Are You?" A slickly authored piece of quasi-detective journalism, Shames's subtitle announced that the author was "In Search of the Beatle Who Spent Two Decades Seeking True Love and Cranial Bliss Only to Discover Cows, Daytime Television, and Palm Beach Real Estate." As Shames surely knew, John and Yoko had become veritable media darlings. Even so, the writer went for broke, framing his narrative as a kind of pop-culture mystery wherein Shames roamed the countryside in search of John, whom he described as "a 40-year-old businessman, who's got $150 million" and "stopped making music." When he couldn't seem to ferret out John's whereabouts, he sought out the prized Holsteins instead, finally locating them in the Catskill Mountains: "Lennon's cows lowed and mooed," Shames wrote, "and I wondered if they had any inkling that their owner had done amazing things a long time ago."[5]

As the *Esquire* article came to a close, Shames reported on the top-secret events at the Hit Factory and the Lennons' impending return to the spotlight. And he even made a sly reference to the "Boston publicity firm [that] is gonna let the news leak out in carefully measured doses."

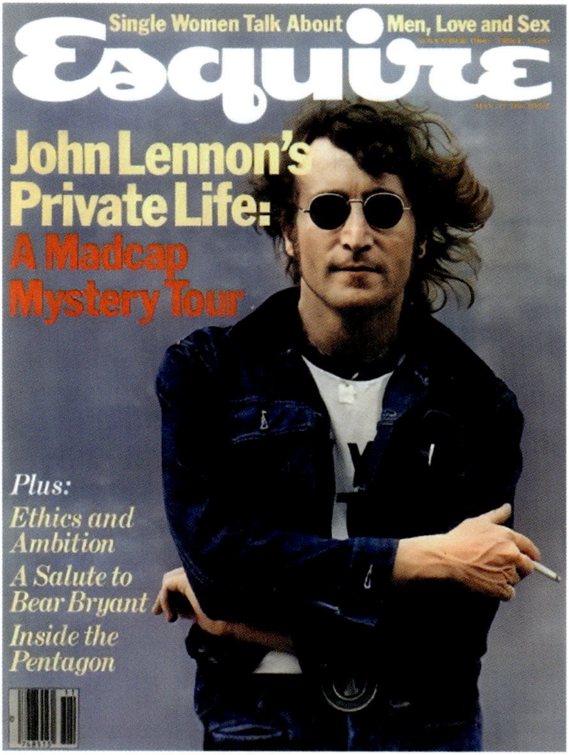

50. *Esquire magazine* cover, November 1, 1980.

A new album was a sure sign of hope, Shames allowed. "With Lennon's eerie stature," he concluded, "you know there's a hit-or-miss genius behind the microphone and maybe, just maybe, something startling will happen."[6] An *Esquire* cover story—even with Shames's mocking perspective—enjoyed a massive reach. The magazine held an international profile, while also drawing a domestic readership that extended throughout the nation—from Alaska to Hawai'i and all across the Lower 48.

Cohen's press release had done its work all right. With the *Esquire* article alighting newsstands the world over and the likes of *Rolling Stone* revving up its music-marketing engine, John and Yoko's latest musical venture was gathering steam. By November, their album's lead single "(Just Like) Starting Over" was climbing up the charts. That same month, *Double Fantasy* was released less than seventy days after Cohen's press release. And even though it didn't immediately set the world on fire, there was no doubt about it: John and Yoko had made good on their August 7 return to the studio. They were back, and the whole world knew it.

Epilogue

Strange Days

On *Double Fantasy*'s "Beautiful Boy (Darling Boy)," John famously sings a lullaby to his five-year-old son Sean, advising him that "life is what happens to you while you're busy making other plans."[1] It was a standout track on an album that was already beginning to capture the public's imagination by the first week of December. The latest *Billboard* charts positioned *Double Fantasy* at number 9, signaling the record's upward trajectory.

Yoko's publicity campaign had shifted into overdrive, including a series of print interviews in *Newsweek* and *Playboy*, as well as prominent BBC and RKO radio engagements. There were plenty of additional PR opportunities on the horizon: prominent English music journalist Ray Connolly was slated to interview John and Yoko at the Dakota on December 9, and a splashy *Rolling Stone* cover story—complete with a spicy Annie Leibovitz photo of a naked Lennon clutching Ono's fully clothed body—was all but certain to make headlines of its own. And Cohen was continuing to work behind the scenes. At one critical juncture, he planted yet another story designed to rehabilitate Yoko's image in *The New York Post* "Page Six" feature. "Yoko told me to start the rumor that a 'secret admirer' was sending her a white rose daily to the Hit Factory," he later recalled.[2]

But everything would change utterly with the awful news coming out of New York City on the evening of December 8. As with millions of television viewers, Farrington would vividly remember the moment in which Howard Cosell interrupted his *Monday Night Football* broadcast to announce that "an unspeakable tragedy confirmed to us by ABC News in New York City. John Lennon, outside of his apartment building on the West Side of New York City, the most famous, perhaps, of all of the Beatles, shot twice in the back, rushed to Roosevelt Hospital, dead on arrival." For Farrington, it was a moment of pure surreality. As the news crisscrossed the globe, he learned that John had been killed just inside the selfsame porte cochere where he had photographed the Lennons scarcely four months earlier on that steamy August afternoon. In disbelief, he tuned his radio to WBCN, Boston's premier rock 'n' roll station, where songs such as "Imagine" were already playing in heavy rotation. "I was all alone and consumed with a deep sadness I had never felt before," he recalled. "I wanted to reach out to someone I could share my immediate grief with, and, after all that we had been through, I instinctively dialed Charles Cohen's office number."

It had been more than a month since the young photographer had tangled with the PR man over the dispensation of Farrington's John and Yoko photos. In spite of the lateness of the hour, he had begun reaching out to the small circle of friends and acquaintances who would share his overriding sense of grief, a sense of despair that was compounded as he imagined the awful tragedy that had befallen Yoko and Sean, their lives forever shattered by a gunman's bullets. Intending to leave a message on Cohen's answering machine, Farrington was startled when the PR man picked up the phone. "Hello, this is Charles Cohen," he announced. "Oh, my God, Charles, can you believe what's happened?" Farrington replied. "Yes, Roger, it is terrible news," Cohen responded rather matter-of-factly with little emotion. "I'm already getting calls from the media," he continued. "Outlets like UPI [United Press International] are all looking for pictures," he paused, as if goading the photographer to answer. "I will be needing photos, Roger," he said. "Can you do that for me, please?"

Farrington was naturally taken aback, having reached out in a time of inconsolable grief only to be rebuffed by Cohen's baser commercial instincts. "This was crazy," Farrington thought to himself. "His request is outrageous and ridiculous. I was under no obligation to him or even Yoko regarding my photos," which the PR man knew that Farrington owned outright. Further, he suspected that Cohen was angry at himself for having neglected to purchase the negatives when he had the chance. Regretting that he had made the call in the first place, Farrington reminded him that he didn't own the images and that the August assignment had long since expired. The very thought that Cohen would capitalize on John and Yoko's personal tragedy was simply too much to bear. Farrington stated the facts, coolly informing him, yet again, that he didn't hold the rights to the thirty-one 8 × 10 numbered prints from the Hit Factory shoot. Farrington, for the first time and after several warnings, knew he had to respond to Cohen's threats by enforcing his copyrights. The PR flak was beside himself, becoming increasingly irate and screaming into the receiver in a cliché-ridden instant, "You'll never work in this city again!"

With his ongoing frustration now piqued to anger, Farrington made two more calls. Knowing that he had to act in the most professional manner to protect his legal rights under the circumstances, he left a message with a local attorney whom he knew from his days at the Charles Playhouse. Farrington clearly needed to register his copyrights for the photos and enforce his ownership with Cohen. His third and final telephone call that evening was to UPI's Beacon Hill office. If Cohen were indeed working with the wire service giant, Farrington knew that he needed to take matters into his own hands—and fast.

Realizing the significance of the moment, UPI's desk editor asked Farrington to meet him at the organization's Ashburton Place offices. "And bring whatever you got," the editor added. And so it was that Farrington found himself with a dozen or so of his John and Yoko prints spread out on a table next to the news agency's Portable Photograph

Transmitter, which conveyed black-and-white and color images via telephone lines. During the short drive over to UPI's offices, Farrington reminded himself that he hadn't intended to capitalize on Lennon's tragic death, merely to assert his copyright in the face of Cohen's ceaseless attempts at taking advantage of him. But at the same time, he realized that his photographs—as some of the last images of the former Beatle—were iconic, historic, and valuable.

Swallowing the lump in his throat and forcing back tears, he agreed to license a trio of photos for UPI's usage. "Whatever shots you choose," the photographer cautioned, "they should definitely include Yoko." When it came to compensation, UPI paid Farrington $5,000—a handsome fee back in those days. Somberly waiting in the agency's offices during the wee hours of the morning, Farrington watched as the photographs were transferred, one by one, line by line, into the Portable Photograph Transmitter. As he sat there, overwhelmed in his grief, Farrington would never forget the sound—zip-zip, zip-zip, zip-zip—as the images disappeared into the ether.

Unbeknownst to Farrington, a similar, albeit far more harrowing scene was playing out in New York City, where Goresh had made the horrifying realization that he had photographed John with his assassin scant hours before the murder. That very afternoon, Goresh had photographed John as he was leaving the Dakota with Yoko for a recording session at the Record Plant, where the couple was putting the finishing touches on "Walking on Thin Ice" with Douglas in the producer's chair. Goresh recalled that the sidewalk along West 72nd Street seemed unusually quiet, prompting John to quip, "Where are my fans?" As always, Goresh was delighted to see his idol. "John looked great that day," the photographer recalled. He had "that Teddy Boy look with the Elvis pompadour." Shortly afterward, another fan walked up, sheepishly extending a copy of *Double Fantasy* and a pen in Lennon's direction. "Do you want me to sign that?" John asked. As he scrawled "John Lennon 1980" across the cover, Goresh snapped a photo of John and the fan, a bespectacled

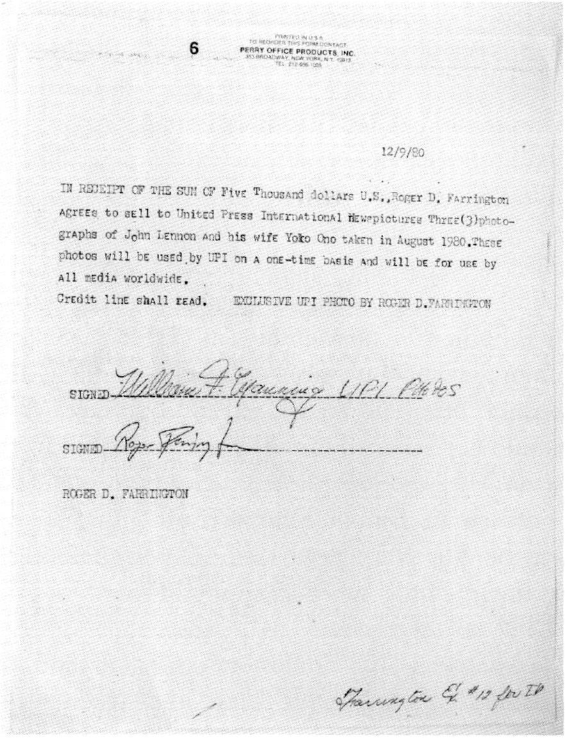

6 PERRY OFFICE PRODUCTS, INC.

12/9/80

IN RECEIPT OF THE SUM OF Five Thousand dollars U.S., Roger D. Farrington agrees to sell to United Press International Newspictures Three(3)photographs of John Lennon and his wife Yoko Ono taken in August 1980.These photos will be used by UPI on a one-time basis and will be for use by All media worldwide.
Credit line shall read. EXCLUSIVE UPI PHOTO BY ROGER D.FARRINGTON

SIGNED William F. [illegible] UPI Photos

SIGNED Roger Farrington

ROGER D. FARRINGTON

Farrington Ex. #12 for ID

51. UPI contract, December 9, 1980.

fellow in a rumpled overcoat. "Is that okay?" John asked, with his eyebrows raised. As the man edged away, John turned back to Goresh and shot him a quizzical look before making the short trip with Yoko over to the Record Plant.[3]

But as it happened, there was nothing innocent about the fan, who lay in wait for John and Yoko's return to the Dakota. Five hours later, he shot and killed Lennon inside the Dakota's Gothic archway. Later that evening, as he learned the tragic news on *Monday Night Football*, Goresh realized that his Minolta XG1 likely held the undeveloped image of John signing an autograph for his killer. Being a good citizen, he attempted to report the photograph's existence to the New York City Police Department. But after the NYPD operator hung up on him for a third time, Goresh spoke with a police sergeant in North Arlington, New Jersey, who recommended that he call the *New York Daily News*. Not missing a beat, the newspaper dispatched a limo to New Jersey to ferry Goresh into the city along with his undeveloped film. The newspaper paid him $10,000 to license the photo, which was one of the final images of John alive. While he was happy to receive the generous compensation, Goresh was tormented with regret at having not recognized the inherent danger in the otherwise unassuming fan. "He looked like the kid that got picked on in the school playground," said Goresh. "He looked like if you blew on him he would have fallen over. If you cracked him in the jaw, he would get knocked out. There was nothing to the guy."[4] For Goresh, selling the notorious photograph didn't result in any repercussions when it came to the Lennon estate. A few months later, when Lennon's "Watching the Wheels" single was released posthumously, Yoko ensured that the amateur photographer's August 7 image of John and her emerging from the Dakota was selected as the cover shot.

Meanwhile, back in Boston, Farrington shortly discovered that Cohen was making good on his threat. That Wednesday, he received a phone call from the *Boston Herald American*'s gossip columnist Norma Nathan, arguably the most feared journalist in Boston. While her "puff pieces" about local big-wigs and celebrities were often perceived as coveted badges of honor—happily received by her subjects and fellow publicists citywide—her merciless personal attacks and penchant for innuendo had ruined plenty of lives when it came to straying politicians, tipsy business notables, visiting celebrities, and a host of local TV and radio personalities. Farrington had made Nathan's acquaintance during his days at the Charles Playhouse, knowing her as a classic Hollywood gossip columnist who played the part exceedingly well. "While black-tied opening night guests sipped champagne amidst clouds of cigarette smoke waiting for the reviews to come in," he later recalled, "there was Norma

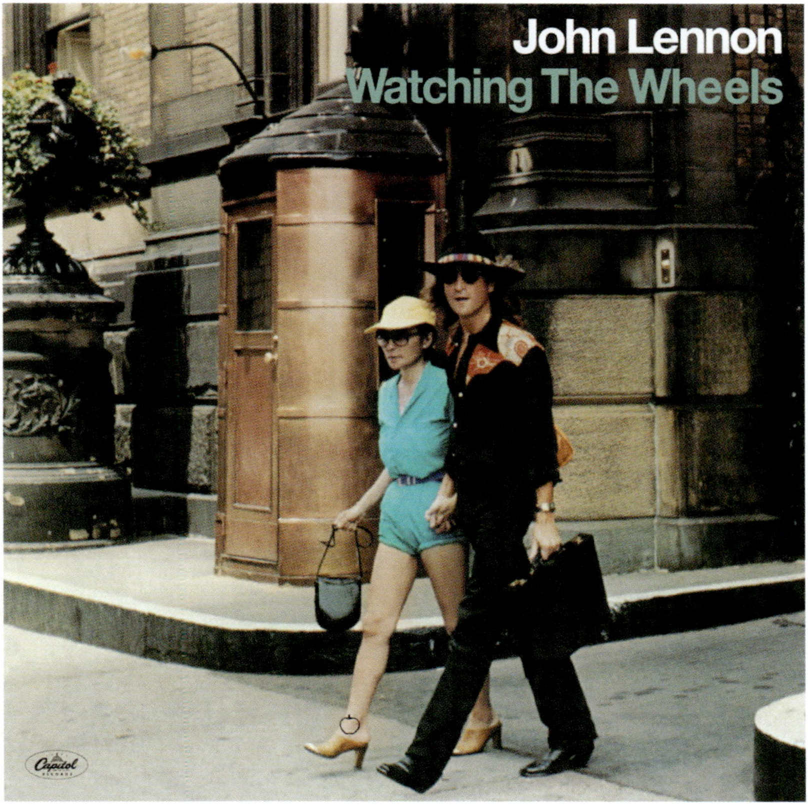

52. "Watching the Wheels" single cover, Geffen Records, March 13, 1981.

Nathan—bright-eyed, round-faced, smiling and frizzled-haired, hopping between guests and stars alike, and always scribbling away on her reporter's notepad. Most folks loved her," he added, "but cautiously kept their distance." Nathan knew that Farrington took photos on Cohen's behalf, who, for his part, was constantly feeding items for the gossip columnist's consideration.

Farrington also understood that *Boston Herald American* journalists—Nathan included—were aware of Cohen's tendency to overembellish on behalf of his clientele. Naturally, when it came to the salacious world of gossip columns, overembellishment and any potential legal fuss often increased readership, rewarding Nathan and her poison pen. For reasons that will become inescapably clear, Farrington would never forget the call, which he received two days after the midnight UPI sale. "Cohen's called Norma Nathan," he reassured himself, "but she knows me. When I give her the facts, she'll know he's just using her, and she'll kill the story, or—better yet—turn against him." Farrington couldn't have been more wrong.

On December 12, the *Boston Herald American* ran Nathan's lead story in which the gossip columnist gleefully took Cohen's side. From Farrington's perspective, the whole sordid business seemed like an underhanded effort by Cohen to besmirch the photographer's reputation as well as an attempt on UPI's part to avoid honoring his contract. "John Lennon's death set off a bitter image scrimmage between freelance Boston photographer Roger Farrington and Charles Cohen, publicist for Yoko Ono," Nathan wrote. "Cohen fired Farrington after the artful Roger tried to sell three very recent photos of Lennon, commissioned by Yoko through Cohen." Of course, Farrington wasn't Cohen's employee per se and hadn't been fired from anything. The job had been completed months ago. But Cohen was only just getting started. "It was cheap, cheap, cheap," an angry Cohen bloviated to Nathan about Farrington's alleged behavior, "to exploit John Lennon's death in direct violation of our understanding. Never were any of those photographs to be sold to anyone at any time."[5]

Within a few weeks, Farrington would receive further evidence about Cohen's level of duplicity when it came to the Hit Factory photographs. On December 23, *Us Weekly* published one of Farrington's photographs of John and Yoko posing along West 48th Street. "Seeing the image in *Us Weekly* confirmed what I already knew," said Farrington. "Cohen had continued to violate his agreement with me that only one image would be selected for news release. Once again, Cohen had pointedly neglected

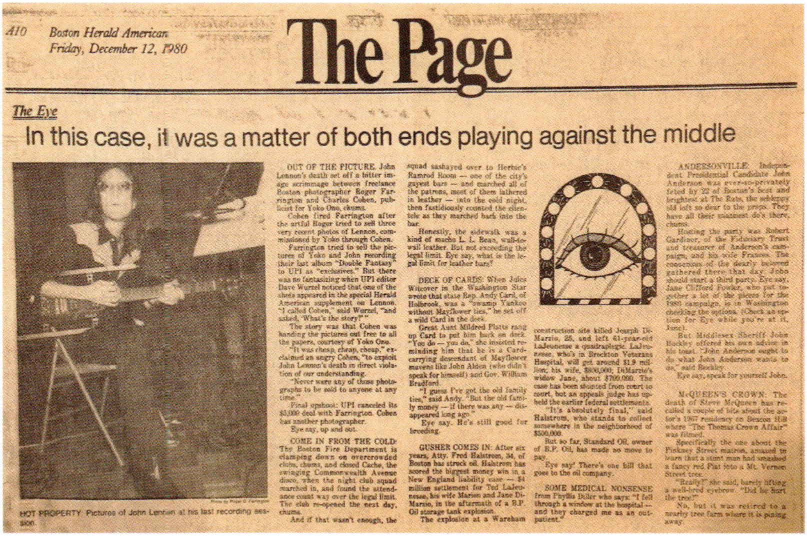

410 Boston Herald American
Friday, December 12, 1980

The Page

The Eye

In this case, it was a matter of both ends playing against the middle

OUT OF THE PICTURE. John Lennon's death set off a bitter image scrimmage between freelance Boston photographer Roger Farrington and Charles Cohen, publicist for Yoko Ono, chums.

Cohen fired Farrington after the artful Roger tried to sell three very recent photos of Lennon, commissioned by Yoko through Cohen.

Farrington tried to sell the pictures of Yoko and John recording their last album "Double Fantasy" to UPI as "exclusives." But there was no fantasizing when UPI editor Dave Wurzel noticed that one of the shots appeared in the special Herald American supplement on Lennon. "I called Cohen," said Wurzel, "and asked, 'What's the story?'"

The story was that Cohen was handing the pictures out free to all the papers, courtesy of Yoko Ono.

"It was cheap, cheap, cheap," exclaimed an angry Cohen, "to exploit John Lennon's death in direct violation of our understanding.

"Never were any of those photographs to be sold to anyone at any time."

Final upshoot: UPI canceled its $5,000 deal with Farrington. Cohen has another photographer.

Eye say, up and out.

COME IN FROM THE COLD: The Boston Fire Department is clamping down on overcrowded clubs, chums, and closed Cache, the swinging Commonwealth Avenue disco, when the night club squad marched in, and found the attendance count way over the legal limit. The club re-opened the next day, chums.

And if that wasn't enough, the squad sashayed over to Herbie's Ramrod Room — one of the city's gayest bars — and marched all of the patrons, most of them lathered in leather — into the cold night, then fastidiously counted the clientele as they marched back into the bar.

Honestly, the sidewalk was a kind of macho L. L. Bean, wall-to-wall leather. But not exceeding the legal limit. Eye say, what is the legal limit for leather bars?

DECK OF CARDS: When Jules Witcover in the Washington Star wrote that state Rep. Andy Card, of Holbrook, was a "swamp Yankee without Mayflower ties," he set off a wild Card in the deck.

Great Aunt Mildred Platts rang up Card to put him back on deck. "You do — you do," she insisted reminding him that he is a Card-carrying descendant of Mayflower mavens like John Alden (who didn't speak for himself) and Gov. William Bradford.

"I guess I've got the old family ties," said Andy. "But the old family money — if there was any — disappeared long ago."

Eye say. He's still good for breeding.

GUSHER COMES IN: After six years, Atty. Fred Halstrom, 34, of Boston has struck oil. Halstrom has scored the biggest money win in a New England liability case — $4 million settlement for Ted LaJeunesse, his wife Marion and Jane DiMarzio, in the aftermath of a B.P. Oil storage tank explosion.

The explosion at a Wareham construction site killed Joseph DiMarzio, 25, and left 61-year-old LaJeunesse a quadraplegic. LaJeunesse, who's in Brockton Veterans Hospital, will get around $1.9 million; his wife, $800,000; DiMarzio's widow Jane, about $700,000. The case has been shunted from court to court, but an appeals judge has upheld the earlier federal settlements.

"It's absolutely final," said Halstrom, who stands to collect somewhere in the neighborhood of $500,000.

But so far, Standard Oil, owner of B.P. Oil, has made no move to pay.

Eye say! There's one bill that goes to the oil company.

SOME MEDICAL NONSENSE from Phyllis Diller who says: "I fell through a window at the hospital — and they charged me as an outpatient."

ANDERSONVILLE: Independent Presidential Candidate John Anderson was ever-so-privately feted by 22 of Boston's best and brightest at The Rats, the schleppy old loft so dear to the preps. They have all their snazziest do's there, chums.

Hosting the party was Robert Gardiner, of the Fiduciary Trust and treasurer of Anderson's campaign, and his wife Frances. The consensus of the dearly beloved gathered there that day: John should start a third party. Eye say, Jane Clifford Fowler, who put together a lot of the pieces for the 1980 campaign, is in Washington checking the options. (Check an option for Eye while you're at it, Jane).

But Middlesex Sheriff John Buckley offered his own advice in his toast. "John Anderson ought to do what John Anderson wants to do," said Buckley.

Eye say, speak for yourself John.

McQUEEN'S CROWN: The death of Steve McQueen has recalled a couple of bits about the actor's 1967 residency on Beacon Hill where "The Thomas Crown Affair" was filmed.

Specifically the one about the Pinkney Street matron, amazed to learn that a stunt man had smashed a fancy red Fiat into a Mt. Vernon Street tree.

"Really?" she said, barely lifting a well-bred eyebrow. "Did he hurt the tree?"

No, but it was retired to a nearby tree farm where it is pining away.

53. Norma Nathan, *Boston Herald American* article, December 12, 1980.

to ask for my permission." But by then, he realized that it was too late. "Cohen and I had gone our separate ways," he lamented, and nothing was seemingly going to change that.

For Farrington, the entire affair had been heartbreaking. Of course, it was a mere trifle in comparison to Lennon's irrevocable loss and his family's ensuing despair. But at the same time, the photographer could not sit idly by while Cohen attacked his integrity in such a public and inflammatory manner. He promptly sued UPI after the news giant canceled its $5,000 agreement with him. In September 1981, Nathan provided her readers with an update on the rancor that existed, and even seemed to be devolving further still, between Farrington and Cohen. "Months after the first suit was filed in Suffolk Superior Court, Farrington is still seething," the gossip columnist wrote, "so much so he has slapped a second suit for $100,000 (for defamation and interference) against Boston publicist Charles Cohen."[6]

Not to be outdone, the PR man claimed to have obtained the services of prestigious Boston law firm Choate, Hall, and Stewart to represent him. With his penchant for hype—even when it came to his own affairs—Cohen boasted that "if we have to, we'll bring on Ono to tell the court that the photographs and negatives Farrington took of her and her late husband were not to be used for any purpose whatsoever unless authorized by me or herself." Even more preposterously, given the state of copyright law vis-à-vis photography, that "the negatives were not the property of Farrington but of Yoko."[7]

For a time, Cohen seemed to have bested Farrington. "You'll never work in this city again," the PR flak had threatened. Cohen's words would echo in the photographer's mind over the next few years. Indeed, for a while Cohen seemed to be making good on his word—at least as far as theatrical and celebrity photography went. But Farrington made do; in those years, there was a growing number of hospitality, retail, and corporate PR events that he had been hired to shoot. And sure enough, Farrington eventually found himself frequently working at the behest of *The Boston Globe* and the *Boston Herald American*, for whom he often submitted photos for the celebrity pages. Eventually, his photographs were appearing regularly in *Boston* magazine and *Town & Country*. Editors across the region rightly perceived Farrington as a photographer who knew how to get the goods—and on deadline, no less. As the 1980s wore on, his spat with Cohen had been all but forgotten. And why not? Any legal doubts had been rendered moot by Ono's affirmation of Farrington's ownership of the copyrights in October 1983. Later, in July 1985, Farrington registered the copyrights with the Library of Congress, earning his profession's ultimate seal of approval.

As for UPI, Farrington's lawsuit took nearly a decade to snake its way through the courts and eventually be settled in his favor as he knew it would. After all, the two parties had a working contract, and Farrington owned the photographs outright. But by that juncture, photojournalism was on the precipice of unprecedented change. When his contract dispute

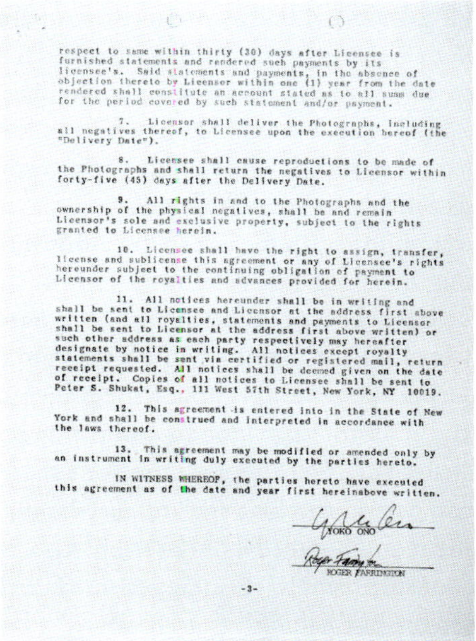

respect to same within thirty (30) days after Licensee is furnished statements and rendered such payments by its licensee's. Said statements and payments, in the absence of objection thereto by Licensor within one (1) year from the date rendered shall constitute an account stated as to all sums due for the period covered by such statement and/or payment.

7. Licensor shall deliver the Photographs, including all negatives thereof, to Licensee upon the execution hereof (the "Delivery Date").

8. Licensee shall cause reproductions to be made of the Photographs and shall return the negatives to Licensor within forty-five (45) days after the Delivery Date.

9. All rights in and to the Photographs and the ownership of the physical negatives, shall be and remain Licensor's sole and exclusive property, subject to the rights granted to Licensee herein.

10. Licensee shall have the right to assign, transfer, license and sublicense this agreement or any of Licensee's rights hereunder subject to the continuing obligation of payment to Licensor of the royalties and advances provided for herein.

11. All notices hereunder shall be in writing and shall be sent to Licensee and Licensor at the address first above written (and all royalties, statements and payments to Licensor shall be sent to Licensor at the address first above written) or such other address as each party respectively may hereafter designate by notice in writing. All notices except royalty statements shall be sent via certified or registered mail, return receipt requested. All notices shall be deemed given on the date of receipt. Copies of all notices to Licensee shall be sent to Peter S. Shukat, Esq., 111 West 57th Street, New York, NY 10019.

12. This agreement is entered into in the State of New York and shall be construed and interpreted in accordance with the laws thereof.

13. This agreement may be modified or amended only by an instrument in writing duly executed by the parties hereto.

IN WITNESS WHEREOF, the parties hereto have executed this agreement as of the date and year first hereinabove written.

YOKO ONO

ROGER FARRINGTON

-3-

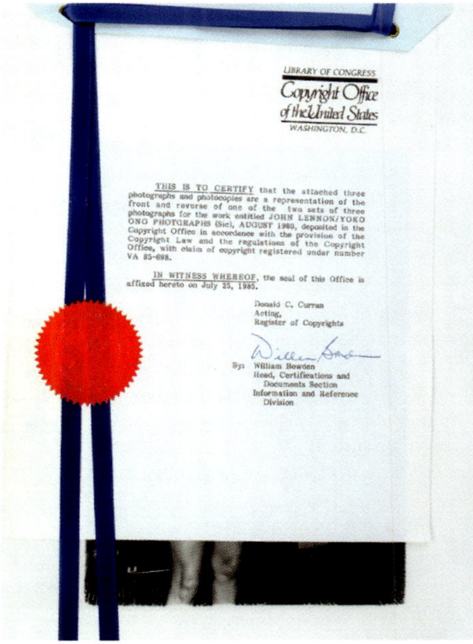

LIBRARY OF CONGRESS
Copyright Office of the United States
WASHINGTON, D.C.

THIS IS TO CERTIFY that the attached three photographs and photocopies are a representation of the front and reverse of one of the two sets of three photographs for the work entitled JOHN LENNON/YOKO ONO PHOTOGRAPHS (Sic), AUGUST 1980, deposited in the Copyright Office in accordance with the provision of the Copyright Law and the regulations of the Copyright Office, with claim of copyright registered under number VA 85-698.

IN WITNESS WHEREOF, the seal of this Office is affixed hereto on July 25, 1985.

Donald C. Curran
Acting,
Register of Copyrights

By: William Bowden
Head, Certifications and Documents Section
Information and Reference Division

54. Yoko Ono copyright agreement, October 24, 1983.
55. Library of Congress copyright registration, July 25, 1985.

came to fruition in 1989, UPI was mired in bankruptcy court—a casualty of an ever-changing industry that would shortly be upended in extraordinary fashion by an encroaching digital age.

Incredibly, Farrington and Cohen's paths crossed several times in the future. And even more remarkably, they came very close to working together again on at least two occasions. In the mid-1980s, Ellie Rosenthal, a Boston PR rep, hatched a bizarre plan with literary agent Ike Williams that called for Farrington and Cohen to collaborate on a book about their misadventures associated with the Hit Factory photos. The photographer agreed to take a meeting with Cohen, Rosenthal, and Williams at a fancy Boston eatery. But almost as soon as Farrington arrived, Cohen began castigating him and making snide remarks. Taking note of Rosenthal's and Williams's wide-eyed response to Cohen's antics, Farrington raised his hands in a pleading gesture. "There he goes again," said the photographer. "It's impossible to work with this guy." Politely excusing himself from the brief meeting, Farrington reminded the parties that he wouldn't be providing access to photos for any project involving his old nemesis.

But their association wasn't over quite yet. In the late 1980s, a Boston-area businessman contacted Farrington about a new PR agency in which he had made a sizable investment. The concept, as he pitched it to Farrington, would involve Cohen leading the agency while Farrington handled the photography. Harboring severe doubts about the project's feasibility, Farrington warned the investor that Cohen could not be trusted. By this juncture, Cohen had managed to alienate the lion's share of his clients. After the businessman persisted in his overtures, Farrington agreed to take part in the experiment and handled a photo shoot associated with a restaurant opening. Not surprisingly, the new venture failed almost as soon as it began. "Cohen's habits had only gotten worse," Farrington lamented. The investor pulled his funding after Cohen proved unable to keep his ego—and his budgetary mismanagement—in check. For his part, Farrington wound up being stiffed for the job.

Seemingly a glutton for punishment but kindhearted to a fault, Farrington made a point of reaching out to Cohen in later years. In 2010, they exchanged convivial emails about their brush with the Lennons in 1980. A few years later, in 2015, Boston's Panopticon Gallery hosted an exhibition of fifty-five of Farrington's celebrity photographs, including six of the Hit Factory images, in commemoration of *Double Fantasy*'s thirty-fifth anniversary. Farrington good-naturedly invited the PR man, who had long since retired, to the opening. Although he ultimately bowed out of the invitation, Cohen—who was now wheelchair-bound—seemed genuinely pleased by the opportunity to bury the hatchet with the photographer lo those many decades later. He died in January 2017 at age seventy-nine.

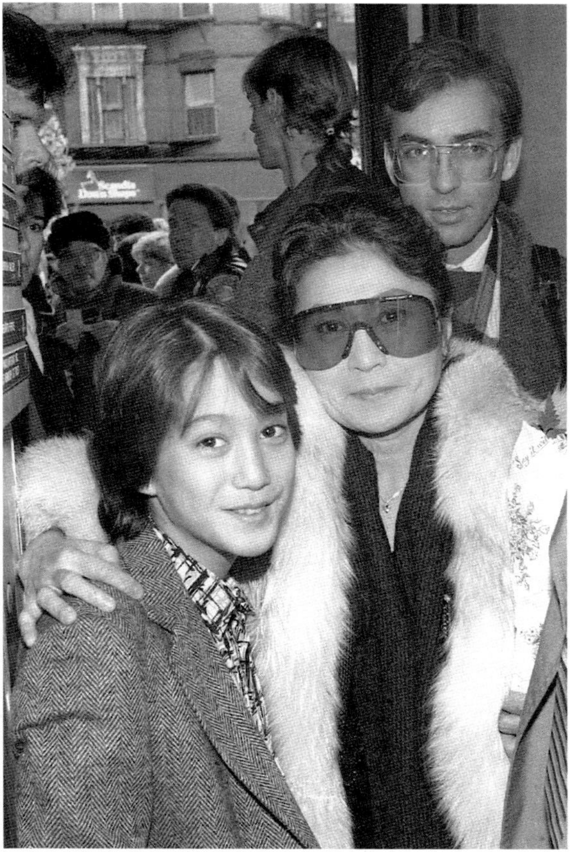

56. Yoko Ono, Sean Ono Lennon, and Sam Havadtoy, Boston, 1985.

Over the course of his long career, Farrington would enjoy the privilege of photographing a movable feast of pop-cultural and historical luminaries, ranging from Cher, John Williams, and Elton John to HRH Prince Charles, Leonard Bernstein, and Frank Sinatra. But nothing would compare to the bittersweet experience of having conducted the Hit Factory photo shoot. If there was any solace for Farrington, it came in the form of Ono's visit to Boston, a few years after her husband's death, for

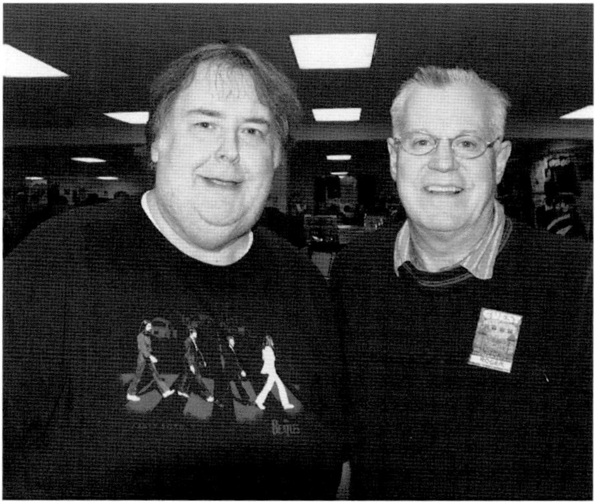

57. Goresh and Farrington at the 2012 Fest for Beatles Fans in Secaucus, New Jersey.

the purposes of attending an art opening at the Ritz-Carlton, which the photographer dutifully covered for the society pages. Cutting a tragic figure in her widowhood, she recognized Farrington from that long ago day in August 1980. She warmly received him and made a point of introducing him to Sean, now in his tenth year. The photographer and his subject had come full circle from those anxiety-ridden moments back at the Hit Factory when John and Yoko seemed to be on the precipice of something much larger and more lasting.

In 1983, when Yoko compiled her *Summer of 1980* anthology, she made sure to include a selection of Farrington's and Goresh's photographs. The compendium pointedly featured images of John in happier times, when the world was brighter and the idea of making music again seemed a worthy cause for coming out of retirement. Her husband had been, as always, a visionary of the highest order, and the photos from that fate-filled summer redound with optimism and hope. Life is indeed what happens to you while you're busy making other plans.

Acknowledgments

This book would not have been possible without a supportive community of friends and colleagues. Special thanks are due to Donald Burnham, Ray Connolly, Joanna Datillo, Wayne Dion, Jack Douglas, Jim Fitts, Ned Farrington, Scott Freiman, Jason Kruppa, Jason Landry, Mark Lewisohn, Chip Madinger, Nicole Michael, Carlee Migliorisi, Andy Nebenzahl, Kit O'Toole, Joe Rapolla, Bruce Replogle, Tim Riley, Ken Sharp, Jeff Slate, Earl Slick, Jon Smith, Steve Valvano, Rich Veit, and Ed Zareh. The irascible Charles Cohen merits particular mention for setting this narrative into motion in the first place. The authors are grateful for the encouragement and advice provided by Peter Mickulas and his production team at Rutgers University Press. We are indebted to the steadfast and loving support of our family members, especially Colleen Babson, Isabel Farrington, and Jeanine Womack.

Notes

Chapter 1

1. Ward Hill Lamon, *Recollections of Abraham Lincoln, 1847–1865* (University of Nebraska Press, 1999), 116–117.
2. Lamon, *Recollections of Abraham Lincoln*, 168.
3. Chip Madinger and Scott Raile, *Lennonology: Strange Days Indeed—A Scrapbook of Madness* (Open Your Books, 2015), 536.
4. John Lennon and Yoko Ono, "John Lennon: The Man, the Memory—Last Interview Special," interview by Dave Sholin and Laurie Kaye, RKO Radio, 1980.
5. Lennon and Ono, "John Lennon."
6. Frederic Seaman, *The Last Days of John Lennon: A Personal Memoir* (Birch Lane, 1991), 158–159.
7. *Camino Real*, by Tennessee Williams, playbill, Provincetown Playhouse (August 1969), provincetownhistoryproject.org/PDF/pil_000_153-provincetown-playhouse-1969.pdf.

Chapter 2

1. Olivia Vanni, "Charles in Charge," *Boston Herald*, December 12, 2010, www.bostonherald.com/2010/12/12/charles-in-charge/.
2. Stephen Birmingham, *Life at the Dakota: New York's Most Unusual Address* (Open Road, 2015), 20.
3. Birmingham, *Life at the Dakota*, 40.
4. In 2017, Ono received a songwriting credit for "Imagine," which had been partially inspired by the poetry in *Grapefruit* (1964), her collection of conceptual-art pieces.
5. The couple's last joint album release was *Some Time in New York City* in June 1972. Yoko's most recent solo LP, *Feeling the Space*, was released in November 1973.

6. Vanni, "Charles in Charge."
7. Released in November 1968, *Unfinished Music No. 1: Two Virgins* was an experimental recording and the result of Lennon and Ono's first professional collaboration. EMI refused to release the controversial album, which was concealed in a brown paper bag and distributed by UK's Track record label. The photograph of John, Yoko, and Sean cavorting in the nude was taken at Cannon Hill, the family's Long Island estate.

Chapter 5

1. Yoko Ono, *John Lennon: Summer of 1980* (Perigee, 1983), 88; Paul Goresh, television interview, 1990, www.youtube.com/watch?v=vgzEDoFTvUY.
2. Goresh, television interview.

Chapter 6

1. Ken Sharp, *Starting Over: The Making of John Lennon and Yoko Ono's Double Fantasy* (Gallery, 2010), 33.
2. Lennon and Ono, "John Lennon."

Chapter 7

1. Brian Kehew, "Flight of the Sardonyx," *Vintage Guitar*, May 2012, 46–47.
2. Jonathan Cott, "John Lennon: The Final Interview," *Rolling Stone*, December 23, 2010, www.rollingstone.com/feature/john-lennon-the-last-interview-179443/.
3. Earl Slick, interview with Kenneth Womack, August 30, 2019; Madinger and Raile, *Lennonology*, 520.
4. Slick, interview.
5. Sharp, *Starting Over*, 29; Jack Douglas, interview with Kenneth Womack, August 11, 2018.
6. The music tech in the background is seventeen-year-old Troy Germano, the son of studio founder Eddie Germano, who purchased and renovated the Hit Factory in 1975.

Chapter 9

1. "Love Fantasy Theme Highlights New John Lennon, Yoko Ono Album: First Album in Seven Years," press release, United Press International, August 12, 1980.
2. Years later, Farrington learned the truth about Yoko's decision to update John's look. In 2012, Farrington attended the Fest for Beatles Fans, where he finally met Goresh in person. The amateur photographer told him that it was John who was chagrinned by his appearance in the Hit Factory images. "I look like Ichabod

Crane!" the ex-Beatle exclaimed. "As soon as they saw the photos," Goresh reported, "Yoko sent him out for a new hairdo." As for the pictures themselves, Goresh added, "I always thought they were great, really great. You got him. The ones in the studio, John playing the guitar, you got really great shots. I wish I had been there."

3. "Random Notes," *Rolling Stone*, September 18, 1980, 31.
4. David Sheff, *Yoko: A Biography* (Simon and Schuster, 2025), 167–168.
5. Laurence Shames, "John Lennon, Where Are You? In Search of the Beatle Who Spent Two Decades Seeking True Love and Cranial Bliss Only to Discover Cows, Daytime Television, and Palm Beach Real Estate," *Esquire*, November 1, 1980, classic.esquire.com/article/1980/11/1/john-lennon-where-are-you.
6. Shames, "John Lennon, Where Are You?"

Epilogue

1. Although Lennon is often credited with crafting this oft-quoted phrase, it was originally coined by Allen Saunders in a January 1957 issue of *Reader's Digest*. John may have seen it in the pages of William Gaddis's 1975 novel *JR*, which was published shortly after the former Beatle's thirty-fifth birthday and was the toast of the New York City literary set at the time. See Kenneth Womack, *John Lennon 1980: The Last Days in the Life* (Omnibus, 2020), 127–128, for further details.
2. Vanni, "Charles in Charge."
3. Sharp, *Starting Over*, 228.
4. Ginger Adams Otis and Graham Rayman, "Paul Goresh, Who Got the Only Picture of John Lennon with His Killer Hours before the Beatle Was Shot, Has Died," *New York Daily News*, April 7, 2018, www.nydailynews.com/2018/01/16/paul-goresh-who-got-only-picture-of-john-lennon-with-his-killer-hours-before-the-beatle-was-shot-has-died/.
5. Norma Nathan, "In This Case, It Was a Matter of Both Sides Playing against the Middle," *Boston Herald American*, December 12, 1980, A10.
6. Norma Nathan, "Lennon Picture Is Bone of Contention," *Boston Herald American*, September 15, 1981, 44.
7. Nathan, "Lennon Picture," 44.

Bibliography

Birmingham, Stephen. *Life at the Dakota: New York's Most Unusual Address*. Open Road, 2015.

Camino Real, by Tennessee Williams. Playbill. Provincetown Playhouse, August 1969. provincetownhistoryproject.org/PDF/pil_000_153-provincetown-playhouse-1969.pdf.

Cott, Jonathan. "John Lennon: The Last Interview." *Rolling Stone,* December 23, 2010. www.rollingstone.com/feature/john-lennon-the-last-interview-179443/.

Goresh, Paul. Television interview, 1990. www.youtube.com/watch?v=vgzEDoFTvUY.

Kehew, Brian. "Flight of the Sardonyx." *Vintage Guitar,* May 2012, 46–47.

Lamon, Ward Hill. *Recollections of Abraham Lincoln, 1847–1865*. University of Nebraska Press, 1999.

Lennon, John, and Yoko Ono. *All We Are Saying: The Last Major Interview with John Lennon and Yoko Ono*. Interview by David Sheff. Edited by G. Barry Golson. Griffin, 2000.

Lennon, John, and Yoko Ono. "John Lennon: The Man, the Memory—Last Interview Special." Interview by Dave Sholin and Laurie Kaye. RKO Radio, 1980.

"Love Fantasy Theme Highlights New John Lennon, Yoko Ono Album: First Album in Seven Years." Press release. United Press International, August 12, 1980.

Madinger, Chip, and Scott Raile. *Lennonology: Strange Days Indeed—A Scrapbook of Madness*. Open Your Books, 2015.

Nathan, Norma. "In This Case, It Was a Matter of Both Sides Playing against the Middle." *Boston Herald American,* December 12, 1980, A10.

Nathan, Norma. "Lennon Picture Is Bone of Contention." *Boston Herald American,* September 15, 1981, 44.

Ono, Yoko. *John Lennon: Summer of 1980*. Perigee, 1983.

Otis, Ginger Adams, and Graham Rayman. "Paul Goresh, Who Got the Only Picture of John Lennon with His Killer Hours before the Beatle Was Shot, Has Died." *New York Daily News,* April 7, 2018. www.nydailynews.com/2018/01/16/

paul-goresh-who-got-only-picture-of-john-lennon-with-his-killer-hours-before-the-beatle-was-shot-has-died/.

"Random Notes." *Rolling Stone,* September 18, 1980, 31.

Seaman, Frederic. *The Last Days of John Lennon: A Personal Memoir*. Birch Lane, 1991.

Shames, Laurence. "John Lennon, Where Are You? In Search of the Beatle Who Spent Two Decades Seeking True Love and Cranial Bliss Only to Discover Cows, Daytime Television, and Palm Beach Real Estate." *Esquire,* November 1, 1980. classic.esquire.com/article/1980/11/1/john-lennon-where-are-you.

Sharp, Ken. *Starting Over: The Making of John Lennon and Yoko Ono's* Double Fantasy. Gallery, 2010.

Sheff, David. *Yoko: A Biography*. Simon and Schuster, 2025.

Vanni, Olivia. "Charles in Charge." *Boston Herald,* December 12, 2010. www.bostonherald.com/2010/12/12/charles-in-charge/.

Womack, Kenneth. *John Lennon 1980: The Last Days in the Life*. Omnibus, 2020.

Illustration Credits

1. *Double Fantasy* album cover, Geffen Records, November 17, 1980 (courtesy of Alamy; photograph by Kishin Shinoyama)
2. *Double Fantasy* sculpture, Bermuda Botanical Gardens (courtesy of Alamy; sculpture by Graham Foster; photograph by Verena Matthew)
3. "Walking on Thin Ice" single cover, Geffen Records, February 6, 1981 (courtesy of Alamy)
4. Roger Farrington, self-portrait, 1983 (courtesy of Roger Farrington)
5. The Charles Playhouse, ca. 1976 (courtesy of Roger Farrington)
6. Jay Leno, Charles J. Cohen, and Frank Sugrue at the Charles Playhouse, 1979 (courtesy of Roger Farrington)
7. The Dakota, 1980 (courtesy of Getty; photograph by Terry Fincher)
8. John, Yoko, and Sean Lennon copy job, July 1980 (courtesy of Roger Farrington)
9. Yoko, John, and the *Double Fantasy* band, September 8, 1980; from left to right: George Small (keyboards), Jack Douglas (producer), George Young (horns), Hugh McCracken (guitar), Tony Levin (bass), Andy Newmark (drums), Earl Slick (guitar), and Howard Johnson (horns) (courtesy of photographer David M. Spindel)
10. Nikon FM camera (courtesy of Roger Farrington)
11. John and Yoko photo 1, August 7, 1980 (courtesy of Roger Farrington)
12. John and Yoko photo 2, August 7, 1980 (courtesy of Roger Farrington)
13. John and Yoko photo 3, August 7, 1980 (courtesy of Roger Farrington)
14. John Lennon and Paul Goresh, November 17, 1980 (courtesy of Alamy, photographer unknown)
15. Goresh photo of Farrington, August 7, 1980 (courtesy of Roger Farrington)
16. John and Yoko photo 4, August 7, 1980 (courtesy of Roger Farrington)
17. John and Yoko photo 5, August 7, 1980 (courtesy of Roger Farrington)
18. John and Yoko photo 6, August 7, 1980 (courtesy of Roger Farrington)
19. John and Yoko photo 7, August 7, 1980 (courtesy of Roger Farrington)

20. John and Yoko photo 8, August 7, 1980 (courtesy of Roger Farrington)
21. John and Yoko photo 9, August 7, 1980 (courtesy of Roger Farrington)
22. John and Yoko photo 10, August 7, 1980 (courtesy of Roger Farrington)
23. John and Yoko photo 11, August 7, 1980 (courtesy of Roger Farrington)
24. John and Yoko photo 12, August 7, 1980 (courtesy of Roger Farrington)
25. John and Yoko photo 13, August 7, 1980 (courtesy of Roger Farrington)
26. John and Yoko photo 14, August 7, 1980 (courtesy of Roger Farrington)
27. Sardonyx advertisement, ca. 1978 (courtesy of Kenneth Womack)
28. John and Yoko photo 15, August 7, 1980 (courtesy of Roger Farrington)
29. John and Yoko photo 16, August 7, 1980 (courtesy of Roger Farrington)
30. John and Yoko photo 17, August 7, 1980 (courtesy of Roger Farrington)
31. John and Yoko photo 18, August 7, 1980 (courtesy of Roger Farrington)
32. John and Yoko photo 19, August 7, 1980 (courtesy of Roger Farrington)
33. John and Yoko photo 20, August 7, 1980 (courtesy of Roger Farrington)
34. John and Yoko photo 21, August 7, 1980 (courtesy of Roger Farrington)
35. John and Yoko photo 22, August 7, 1980 (courtesy of Roger Farrington)
36. John and Yoko photo 23, August 7, 1980 (courtesy of Roger Farrington)
37. John and Yoko photo 24, August 7, 1980 (courtesy of Roger Farrington)
38. John and Yoko photo 25, August 7, 1980 (courtesy of Roger Farrington)
39. John and Yoko photo 26, August 7, 1980 (courtesy of Roger Farrington)
40. John and Yoko photo 27, August 7, 1980 (courtesy of Roger Farrington)
41. John and Yoko photo 28, August 7, 1980 (courtesy of Roger Farrington)
42. John and Yoko photo 29, August 7, 1980 (courtesy of Roger Farrington)
43. John and Yoko photo 30, August 7, 1980 (courtesy of Roger Farrington)
44. John and Yoko photo 31, August 7, 1980 (courtesy of Roger Farrington)
45. John and Yoko negatives, August 7, 1980 (courtesy of Roger Farrington)
46. John and Yoko contact sheet, August 8, 1980 (courtesy of Roger Farrington)
47. Advertising and Entertainment transmittal page, August 12, 1980 (courtesy of Roger Farrington)
48. Advertising and Entertainment press release, August 12, 1980 (courtesy of Roger Farrington)
49. *Rolling Stone*, "Random Notes," September 18, 1980 (courtesy of Roger Farrington)
50. *Esquire* magazine cover, November 1, 1980 (courtesy of Kenneth Womack; original photograph by Bob Gruen)
51. UPI contract, December 9, 1980 (courtesy of Roger Farrington)
52. "Watching the Wheels" single cover, Geffen Records, March 13, 1981 (courtesy of Alamy; photograph by Paul Goresh)

53. Norma Nathan, *Boston Herald American* article, December 12, 1980 (courtesy of Roger Farrington)
54. Yoko Ono copyright agreement, October 24, 1983 (courtesy of Roger Farrington)
55. Library of Congress copyright registration, July 25, 1985 (courtesy of Roger Farrington)
56. Yoko Ono, Sean Ono Lennon, and Sam Havadtoy, Boston, 1985 (courtesy of Roger Farrington)
57. Goresh and Farrington at the 2012 Fest for Beatles Fans in Secaucus, New Jersey (courtesy of Roger Farrington, photographer unknown)

About the Authors

ROGER FARRINGTON is a Boston-based publicity photographer. His images have appeared in publications worldwide including *Time, Newsweek, People, Parade, Vogue, Town & Country, The New York Times, The Washington Post, Paris Match,* and *The Boston Globe*. In addition to his iconic 1980 images of John Lennon and Yoko Ono, Roger Farrington has photographed numerous celebrities, including Andy Warhol, HRH Prince Charles, Matt Damon, Cher, Richard Pryor, Elton John, Jay Leno, Alec Baldwin, Dionne Warwick, Cyndi Lauper, Luciano Pavarotti, Frank Sinatra, Michael Douglas, Danny DeVito, Charlton Heston, Liza Minnelli, Billy Joel, Vanna White, John Williams, Leonard Bernstein, Seiji Ozawa, and many others. His work has been exhibited in Boston, New York City, Liverpool, and Tokyo.

KENNETH WOMACK is one of the world's foremost writers and thinkers about the Beatles. He is the author of the acclaimed two-volume biography devoted to the life and work of Beatles producer George Martin, including *Maximum Volume* and *Sound Pictures*. His most recent Beatles-related works include the bestselling books *Solid State: The Story of Abbey Road and the End of the Beatles, John Lennon 1980: The Last Days in the Life,* and *Living the Beatles Legend: The Untold Story of Mal Evans*. Over the years, he has served as an expert commentator for ABC's *20/20*, MSNBC's *Morning Joe*, and NBC's *Access Hollywood*. He is a professor of English and popular music at Monmouth University.